Designing UX: Forms

by Jessica Enders

Copyright © 2016 SitePoint Pt

Managing Editor: Simon Mackie

Series Editor: Joe Leech

English Editor: Ralph Mason

Technical Edito ...

Cover Designer: Alex Walker

Illustrator: Natalia Balska

Published by SitePoint Pty. Ltd.

48 Cambridge Street Collingwood
VIC Australia 3066
Web: www.sitepoint.com
Email: books@sitepoint.com

ISBN 978-0-9943470-5-3 (print)

ISBN 978-0-9953826-0-2 (ebook)
Printed and bound in the United States of America

About Jessica Enders

Jessica Enders has suffered from a lifelong condition known as a love of designing forms, applications and other transactional interfaces. She is attempting to minimize the adverse symptoms by running her own form design business, Formulate Information Design[1]. Formulate's international clients include PayPal and the Mayo Clinic; in Australia, Jessica has worked across all sectors for organizations such as Wesfarmers, Coles, Diabetes Australia, Sydney Water, Royal Melbourne Hospital, VicRoads and the Australian Prudential Regulation Authority.

Jessica has two decades of award-winning, unbeatable return-on-investment form design experience. If you have a problem with completion/conversion rates, poor data quality, low customer satisfaction or high incidence of user error, Jessica knows how to fix it. She also believes in sharing her insights with clients and community alike, writing and presenting widely. This book is her latest step toward making the world a better place, one well-designed form at a time.

About SitePoint

SitePoint specializes in publishing fun, practical, and easy-to-understand content for web professionals. Visit http://www.sitepoint.com/ to access our blogs, books, newsletters, articles, and community forums. You'll find a stack of information on JavaScript, PHP, Ruby, mobile development, design, and more.

---

[1] http://www.formulate.com.au/

For m.e.

You are my everything.

Table of Contents

Preface

Have you ever had a debate with your team about whether a form label should go above, inside or to the left of its field? Or whether or not to disable a button until all the required fields are filled out? Maybe a stakeholder wants to include a dumb question, and you need to help them see the light.

This book is here to help. You'll find the answers to all of the above and much more, as we look at the factors behind great form experience. It's an easy read from cover to cover, but the book is also divided into sections with clear headings that make it simple to jump to specific information.

We will concentrate on designing mobile-friendly, accessible web forms, but the focus on underlying principles means plenty is applicable to other types of forms—such as mobile and desktop apps, kiosks and even paper forms. You'll learn best practice for visual design, how to write effective questions, and what makes for a smooth flow, with some tips about managing form design projects as a bonus. So join me as we refashion forms from frustrating to fabulous.

Who Should Read This Book

This book is for designers, developers, aspiring UX professionals, and anyone with an interest in building forms that work beautifully.

Conventions Used

Look out for the following items.

Tips, Notes, and Warnings

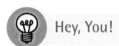 Hey, You!

Tips provide helpful little pointers.

Ahem, Excuse Me ...

Notes are useful asides that are related—but not critical—to the topic at hand. Think of them as extra tidbits of information.

Make Sure You Always ...

... pay attention to these important points.

Watch Out!

Warnings highlight any gotchas that are likely to trip you up along the way.

Supplementary Materials

- https://www.sitepoint.com/community/ are SitePoint's forums, for help on any tricky web problems.
- **books@sitepoint.com** is our email address, should you need to contact us to report a problem, or for any other reason.

Chapter **1**

Introduction

I hate telling people what I do.

Usually, the response is one of confusion: blank looks and pregnant pauses. I go on to explain, "You know, like when you have to register your car or be admitted to hospital: I design the form you fill out, so it's less painful." Some understanding is restored using these everyday examples. Yet people are still surprised to learn that someone actually designs these forms (a depressingly apt reflection on the quality of most).

Designing Forms Is the Worst Best Job in the World

Surprising as it may be, I love what I do. As it draws on so many different subject areas, designing forms is one of the most interesting professions you can have. It's kinda like getting paid to solve rewarding puzzles that make other people's lives easier.

And boy are there a lot of puzzles out there that need solving. After all, when was the last time you heard someone gush with delight about a wonderful form they just filled out? Instead, every day, forms make people want to pull their hair out in frustration. And every day, organizations waste millions of dollars collecting information poorly.

But despite the huge need, and the fascinating, diverse work, form design isn't a recognized discipline. If you tell people you're an accountant, or a landscaper, or even a web developer, they have an inkling of what you do. Form design, on the other hand, is a niche within the niche of user experience.

It shouldn't be this way. The world needs more people who understand what makes one form easier to fill out than another. For some of you, reading this book will light a spark that sets you on the path to becoming a specialist form designer. For most of you, however, it'll mean you're a bit more prepared to design the form that's part of a bigger web project. And while you may not be boisterously celebrated for the functional and aesthetic form you produce, know that you've made a real, tangible difference both to the people filling it out, and to your organization. Besides, at the end of the day, nothing happens without a form.

Some (Crucial) Definitions

You'd be hard pressed to find professions that ruminate about definitions more than User Experience and Design. But I'm rather inclined to go against the grain, and this is meant to be a *practical* book, so I'm just going to tell you straight up what you need to know.

In this book:

- A **form** is any physical interface that collects information from at least one party, and delivers it to at least one other party, so that a product or service can be provided. A form can be on paper, on a mobile, within a complex desktop application, or even a bank's automatic teller machine (ATM).

A **web form** is a form that people fill out inside the browser, and is the only kind of form we're going to cover in this book (although many of the techniques can be used with other types of forms). It has its basis in HTML, CSS and JavaScript, but may be built using:

- a front-end framework such as Twitter's Bootstrap
- a CSS preprocessor like Sass or Less
- JavaScript libraries like jQuery
- programming languages such as PHP and Ruby on Rails[1].

A **user** is someone who is filling out your form. It's a regular person, who may be internal or external to your organization. Yes, "user" isn't an especially elegant term, but it's simpler than "form filler", so I'm sticking with it.

The **target audience** is the group of users for whom the form applies, as a whole. Sometimes the target audience can be segmented into groups according to things like characteristics, motivations, preferences or demographics.

The **form owner** is the organization that creates the form, to collect some necessary information, from the target audience. Within the organization, there will be many people who have a stake in the form—the **stakeholders**—but hopefully there's one person who has the ultimate decision-making authority—the **project owner**.

User experience is the experience users have when they use something. In our case, it refers to the experience they have when they fill out your form. *Our aim is to create an optimal user experience*, such that the needs of both the users and the form owner are met.

Design means the choices we make about how our form will look, feel and work. It doesn't matter what your actual job title is, or whether you've ever studied design. If you're writing words, setting out text boxes or coding up a button, you're doing design.

[1.] Don't worry if you don't know anything about these programming languages. You won't need to for the purposes of this book.

Research refers to learning about the needs, wants, contexts, preferences and opinions of both users and stakeholders. To some extent, all user experience research techniques[2] are applicable to forms. But the most relevant are:

- **contextual enquiry** (observing and interviewing users in the situation where the form would be filled)
- **analytics review** (examining form metrics and samples of completed forms, to see where things are going wrong)
- **usability testing** (watching people fill out a form to see what's working and what isn't)[3]
- **A/B testing** (a controlled experiment to see which of two design options for a particular element performs best).

There's also a specialist technique for form research called **cognitive interviewing**, which is a combination of contextual enquiry and user testing tailored for the form-filling context. It was developed out of social psychology, for testing survey questionnaires. If you're interested in learning more about cognitive interviewing, a place to start is the "How To" guide by Gordon Willis[4].

Three Dimensions

Every form has three dimensions (from relatively most to least influential for user experience)[5]:

1. **Words** (what you say in the form, and how you say it)
2. **Layout** (how things are presented, visually)

[2.] http://uxmastery.com/resources/techniques/

[3.] Sometimes people call this "user testing", but usability testing better conveys that it's not the user that's being tested, it's the interface.

[4.] http://www.hkr.se/pagefiles/35002/gordonwillis.pdf

[5.] Technically speaking, I also talk about a fourth dimension: **Process**. Process is everything that happens *around* the form itself, from how people get access to it, to what happens after it's submitted, and all the associated organizational activity. Process can also significantly influence user experience, but is beyond the scope of this book. Having said that, you're likely to uncover opportunities for process improvement just by following the techniques we discuss, especially those specific to managing a forms project (Chapter 2).

3. **Flow** (how the user moves through the form).

You'll probably find form design more manageable if you can get a firm sense of these three dimensions. They'll help ensure you've considered all key components, and will provide a common language for discussions with colleagues and peers. The dimensions can also provide a framework for the planning and division of work, as well as pinpointing where design problems are occurring. Finally, it's just too damn overwhelming to try to design all three dimensions at once!

Correspondingly, the core of this book is divided into three major chapters—one for each dimension—plus a brief summary of managing form projects:

- Chapter 2: Form Projects
- Chapter 3: Words
- Chapter 4: Layout
- Chapter 5: Flow.

Which Forms This Book Is About

Before we get too much further into detail, we should further clarify *which* forms this book is about.

Online

Would you design a novel the same way you'd design an advertising billboard? Surely not, as the medium influences the design. The constraints and goals also differ.

The same is true for forms. While there are some commonalities, forms designed for paper follow different rules from those designed for digital. And within digital, designing a native app for an Android smartphone is very different from designing an enterprise system to run on the desktop. Furthermore, what defines a native app today—let alone what operating system the app is native to—may have changed by tomorrow.

If we tried to cover all these different types of forms, as well as all the aspects of good form design, your head would explode. (Plus, researching, writing and designing a book takes a lot of work, so I want it to be valid for more than two minutes!)

So we're going to focus on the most adaptable, accessible and durable type of form: web forms. As we defined earlier, web forms are those that run in the browser (e.g. Google Chrome or mobile Safari on the iPhone) and are based on HTML, CSS, and JavaScript.

This is a book about *designing* forms, though, so you don't need to understand these programming languages, or coding generally. Rather, all the rationale and recommendations apply to web forms, but may not carry across directly to other contexts.

We'll dip into HTML from time to time, where it's relevant for enhancing the user experience. And if you don't have any familiarity with programming for the web, SitePoint has some great places to start, such as the free *Build Your First Website: HTML & CSS*[6] course by Russ Weakley.

Mobile

One of the reasons I declare web forms to be the most adaptable is that they work on mobiles, tablets and other small screens *as well as* laptops, desktops and TVs. In fact, this is one of the real advantages of web forms: **you can design a single form that will *respond* to the screen size**.

Consequently, in this book you won't find any chapters specifically on "mobile form design". Instead **we're going to produce one design that works everywhere**. In other words, we're going to do *responsive form design*. This is much better than having to come up with multiple designs that each need to be developed and maintained, right?

In fact, the great news is that most of the design approaches work for all screen sizes, without any particular modification. The key exceptions—which we'll point out as we go along—are:

[6.] https://www.sitepoint.com/premium/courses/build-your-first-website-html-css-2891

- label placement
- text sizes
- buttons.

Touch

As Josh Clark says in the introduction to his great book *Designing for Touch*[7]:

> For decades, we explored the digital world with prosthetics called mouse, keyboard and cursor. We nudged plastic bricks across our desks. We directed onscreen arrows to poke buttons from afar. We clicked icons. We pointed at pixels. But then we started holding those pixels in our hands. Thanks to smartphones, billions of people wrangle touch screens every day, all day.

It's no longer enough to design our forms so that they work just with mouse and keyboard. We have to accommodate fingers and thumbs, too. But touch, as a way of interacting with an interface, is not clearly associated with a particular environment, unlike screen size, operating system or device type. We can never really know when our form will be filled out using touch. **Thus, we must make all our forms touch-friendly by default.**

If you don't know much about touch, here are some key tips:

- Touch can be found on all sizes of screen, from small smartphones to large display monitors. So don't use screen size as an indicator of touch.
- The minimum touch target size is 7mm, which equates to 44 pixels (or points or dp).
- For responsive designs, this equates to 2.75 rems (a "rem" is a "root em"—see "Font sizing with rem"[8]).
- There's no such thing as "hover" on a touch device, so try to avoid using it in your designs.
- Fewer taps are better, as arms, hands and wrists get sore easily.

And if all of that is way too technical for you, just pass it on to your developers!

[7.] https://abookapart.com/products/designing-for-touch
[8.] https://snook.ca/archives/html_and_css/font-size-with-rem

Accessibility

The same applies to accessibility. Instead of trying to retrofit accessibility to our form after the fact, or try to apply it in a subset of use cases, we're going to **bake accessibility right into our design**. After all, accessibility "features"—like readable text and colors that don't clash—help all users, not just those with disabilities.

Performance

As web technology has evolved, web pages have grown in size (or weight, depending on how you like to think about it). Larger pages take longer to load, and slow-loading pages certainly detract from user experience. True, internet connectivity and mobile networks have also improved. But these improvements struggle to keep pace with the evolution of the web. The improvements are also not evenly distributed—as people from rural areas to inner city black spots can tell you, not to mention other countries.

Ideally, we should aim to create forms that load and respond comparatively fast, using familiar, straightforward, standards-compliant design approaches, and keeping our forms free from many of the things that increase the size of web pages, such as advertisements. (See <u>"What's Absent from Our Layout"</u> in Chapter 4.)

One Design to Rule Them All

In summary, this book will show you how to design a form that will:

- work on the web—on all devices (including mobile), and regardless of browser or operating system
- be responsive to screen size
- suit touch, in addition to the more traditional input devices of mouse and keyboard
- be accessible to people of all abilities, including those using assistive technologies like screen readers and magnifiers
- load quickly, and respond quickly to user interaction.

What Makes a Good Form?

Imagine we were to create this one design to rule them all. How would we know that it's actually *good*?

Frank Pick is famous for transforming the London Underground from "a mild form of torture" to "the most famous and respected transport system in the world"[9]. In 1916, he is quoted as saying:

> The test of the goodness of a thing is its fitness for use. If it fails on this first test, no amount of ornamentation or finish will make it any better; it will only make it more expensive, more foolish.

When it comes to a form, being "fit for use" means that it **collects information that an organization needs, within context, while also catering for the needs and context of users.**

As you can see from this definition:

- collecting information is what sets forms apart from other types of interaction
- a form is only as good as the knowledge you have about the specific needs and context of both *your* users and *your* organization.

I've helped organizations collect information for 20 years. This book represents the core of what I've learned in that time, and will take you a long way toward efficient, effective and satisfying forms. But because every need and context is unique, your forms will only be great with research.

It's beyond the scope of this book to explore research. Instead, I'll mention when it will especially help to draw on the key techniques mentioned earlier:

- contextual enquiry
- analytics review
- usability testing
- A/B testing.

[9.] http://distortedarts.com/lives-frank-pick/

For those interested in further information, these and other techniques are covered extensively elsewhere, in books like *Observing the User Experience, Second Edition: A Practitioner's Guide to User Research* by Goodman, Kuniavsky and Moed and *Usability Testing Essentials: Ready, Set...Test!* by Carol Barnum, and websites bursting with resources, like SitePoint[10] and UX Mastery[11]. Also keep an eye out for future design, planning and research books in the SitePoint *Aspects of UX* series, of which this is the first release.

Now that we've established what a form is, which forms we're talking about, and what makes a form good, in the next chapter we'll focus briefly on form design projects, before diving deeper into the meaty details of form design.

---

[10]. https://www.sitepoint.com/design-ux/
[11]. http://uxmastery.com/

Chapter 2

Form Projects

General project management techniques apply when working on forms as much as any other web venture. There's a raft of information available on such techniques, and in all likelihood your organization or team have already selected what works well for them.

Given this, and the fact that I'm certainly no project management expert, we won't discuss any standard approaches here. What I will share is what I've found works well on my form projects with clients, namely:

- gathering form-specific information
- assessing metrics of existing forms
- refraining from copying forms on other sites
- establishing an overarching, guiding principle for form design.

Form-specific Information Gathering

Regardless of whether you're following a waterfall or agile project methodology, I find it highly informative to ask the following questions at the very start of the project.

Questions to Ask

Questions that apply regardless of whether or not the form you're designing is completely new, or will be replacing one or more existing forms:

- What are you trying to achieve by designing this form?
- What are the three most common scenarios for its use?
- Who is the target audience?
- How will the new form relate to the organization's goals?
- What constraints are there (including existing style guides and choices around technology)?
- Where will the form fit within overall business processes?
- How will the form relate to other digital or paper-based systems (including forms)?
- How will user support be provided?
- How will the form affect the following activities of the organization, and vice versa?
  - IT
  - policy
  - operations
  - sales
  - marketing
  - legal
- Might the form need any of the following (all of which add considerable complexity to any form project, and are beyond the scope of this book)?
  - real-time processing (as opposed to batch)
  - "wet" (i.e. handwritten) signature(s)
  - electronic signature(s)
  - authentication or identity management

- workflow management (e.g. multiple form fillers, processors, delegates, or approvers)
- online payment
- offline payment
- supporting documents or attachments
- Are there existing forms that will be modified or replaced by the form you're designing?

If there are existing forms, try to gather:

- current and previous versions (so you can see how it has evolved over time)
- metrics, at least for the current version (see below)
- any supporting documentation (e.g. records of version numbers and changes, user research findings).

What If You're Doing Agile Development or Lean UX?

Agile development[1] is characterized by a focus on the iterative delivery of working software, by a collaborative, cross-disciplinary, customer-focused team. Scrum is the main method that organizations currently use to implement agile.

"Customer focus" is just another way of saying **user experience**. While the agile principles put customer focus front and center, in reality it can often fall by the wayside. This is why it's good to have a methodology for ensuring user experience is built into the development process. Lean UX is one such methodology.

While strictly speaking *not* a feature of agile, some form designers find they still need to do a discovery phase before any sprints commence. The discovery phase is where you should try to gather at least a high-level set of answers to the questions above, even if the detail isn't going to be worked out until the sprints themselves. You could think of this discovery phase as "informed assumptions" (assumptions being a foundation of agile processes).

In practice, the development of forms, using approaches like agile, scrum and lean, is still relatively new.

---

[1] http://www.agilemanifesto.org/principles.html

What If the Form Is Part of a Bigger Web Project?

Often, the form is just one component of a bigger site. Just as often, the form is an afterthought, and offers a terrible user experience.

In fact, because forms have:

- the greatest level of interactivity
- unique elements
- a real impact on the operations of the organization

they must be considered *as early as possible*. Also, a single form is likely to need as much resources as multiple pages on an informational website. If the form is long or complex, it may need exponentially more.

How to Ask

If you can, ask these questions face to face. You'll glean more nuggets than if you asked by phone, email or survey—even if just because it's easier to probe when face to face.

Who to Ask

These questions should be asked of the project owner and stakeholders (see "Some (Crucial) Definitions" in Chapter 1), ideally on a one-to-one basis. That way, you'll be able to tell whether or not all parties are on the same page, and proactively manage any differences. Such differences often have very little to do with the form and a great deal to do with organizational politics and culture.

As the form's designer, you may not be especially comfortable dealing with these differences, but it's imperative you do what you can to bring them to the fore, as soon as possible. Otherwise, they can snowball into conflicts that have serious impacts on user experience.

For instance, I once was hired as the consulting designer on a project where the legal team were involved as part of the project board, but not sufficiently briefed when the IT team made some key decisions about the structure of the form. These decisions in turn influenced the form's flow and words.

The design had progressed all the way through to development, and on to final user acceptance and performance testing, before legal were brought in again, to "sign off". Unfortunately, legal felt there were serious issues with the structure, and disallowed it. This meant the whole form had to be shoehorned into the technology framework that had been set up, and hasty changes made to the flow and words. The final product was not a cohesive, seamless user experience.

This project and the outcome would have been much more successful if legal had been involved throughout the design process. Alas, neither the project owner nor legal could be convinced to do this.

This project also serves to illustrate the importance of stakeholder involvement. Nobody likes surprises, and stakeholders are no different. It's quite possible that one of the reasons legal were unhappy with the chosen structure was because it was unexpected, and they felt left out. It certainly wasn't the only project I've seen where insufficient stakeholder consultation led to designs being rejected late in the process. (When you're an external consultant, you aren't always able to connect with stakeholders as much as you'd like.)

Metrics

If one or more existing forms are going to be replaced or supplemented by the form you're designing, you should collect the following data about those forms:

Usage:

- visit rate (for web forms)
- download rate (for paper or PDF forms downloaded from the web)
- print count (for paper forms that your organization prints for users).

Conversion/completion rates:

- at question, section and step/screen level
- split by target audience segment, if possible (see "Some (Crucial) Definitions" in Chapter 1).

Time to complete:

split by target audience segment, if possible.

Error rates:

at question, section and step/screen level
split by target audience segment, if possible.

User satisfaction:

split by target audience segment, if possible.

Costs:

printing
storage
distribution
data
hosting
licensing
processing.

These metrics will become your "before" measure, so you can later demonstrate the value of good form design.

Even if there aren't any existing forms, you want to set the environment up so that these metrics can be collected for the new form you're designing.

Metrics Can Highlight Design Issues

The metrics from any existing forms should also influence the design you're doing now. Look for the following, which indicate there might be a problem with the user experience:

low usage, completion rates, and user satisfaction
high time to complete, error rates, and costs

Of course, metrics will tell us *what* is happening, but not *why*. In some cases, you'll be able to spot ways in which the form doesn't follow best practices in this book. But because each context is different, you may well need to do user research to uncover what's causing poor results.

Don't Copy Others

In all of the above, you'll see I don't mention researching how other organizations design their forms. This is because a minuscule number of forms are well designed, and even fewer are properly researched with users. This is why most people hate forms.

If you copy an existing form, all you'll be doing is replicating a bad design. Much better to create your own good design by using the techniques in this book, all of which have been validated with users, at one time or another.

The one exception to this is a strongly established convention, like collecting username before password on a log in form. Precisely because such conventions are so strongly established, we stray from them at our peril. Usually, it's only the big guns, like Apple and Google, who can get away with designs that disrupt convention.

But even for them it doesn't always work. With iOS 7, the operating system for iPhones and iPads from late 2013, Apple moved starkly away from the use of visual elements to communicate with users. Instead, Apple relied on just text, together with users' familiarity with previous iOS versions, to convey how their interfaces worked.

iOS 6   iOS 7

2-1. An example of the loss of visual cues between iOS 6 and iOS 7: the back button

2-2. Another example of the loss of visual cues between iOS 6 and iOS 7: form buttons

As my skeptical peers will attest, I predicted this change would cause usability issues, and indeed it did. As Josh Clark describes in his book *Designing for Touch*[2]:

> Experienced Apple users knew how these flattened widgets functioned from past versions, but newcomers faced precious few visual clues. Widgets still behaved with physicality—sliders slide, cards flipped—but figuring out that they were sliders or cards was trial and error. Worse, the flattening of the interface also squashed the discoverability of basic elements, even buttons.

Apple has since enabled the return of outlines to buttons, but doggedly stuck with some other text-only styling, perhaps because they think they have enough market share to do what they like. The rest of us should heed this cautionary tale about messing with established conventions.

A Guiding Principle for Form Design

At this stage of your form project, you've got an awful lot of information about what's been happening, and hopefully some insight into what's not working. Before you jump into design—and the heart of this book—I want to put you in the right mindset.

Charles Holden worked with Frank Pick on the London Underground, and is credited as having said:

> Eliminate everything which does not fulfill a definite and necessary function.

[2.] https://abookapart.com/products/designing-for-touch

This advice applies well to forms, but in fact I would go a step further and say:

> **Start with nothing. Then only add what's needed to communicate with the user.**

The "nothing" you start with is a blank screen. No words, no color, no shape. **Every single pixel you add should be necessary to guide the user experience.** And every time someone asks you to put more in, ask them, and ask yourself, "Will this aid the user, and if so, how?" If it's going to be solely for the organization's benefit, or doesn't tell the user anything new, don't include it.

Be ruthless.

Be brave.

And be ready, for now you're going to start designing your form.

Chapter

3

Words

This chapter is all about the words you use in your forms. They're the most influential component of your design—more so than how your form looks.

Do come for a stroll through the world of words with me, and see just how much they can do.

Words Matter Most

A web form is a text-driven interface. The core of the interaction is the questions asked and answers given. This is why the *words* we use in the form—and *not* how it looks—are the **most important part of the design**.

Have a look at the image below. This ecommerce form has an attractive, clean layout. But can you fill it out? The heading talks of checking whether the item is available *in store*. Yet the question itself refers to *delivery*. The waters are muddied even more by the instruction: "Please enter your local post code to check availability".

3-1. The words, not the layout, make this form hard to fill out

Now let's create a version of this form that has an awful layout (see Chapter 4 for details of what's wrong) but clear wording. While this might not be the prettiest form you'll ever see, you'll still be able to complete it:

3-2. If the words are right, users can work around bad layout

Questions

As we noted above, the core of a form is the questions we ask. They are what distinguish a form from other types of web interfaces. So if we want the user experience of our form to be good, we need to write good questions.

How hard can writing a good question be? After all, every day we're asking (and answering) questions: "Any sugar in your coffee?" ... "When will the testing happen?" ... "What's for dinner?" These exchanges require hardly any effort or conscious thought.

Good Form Questions Are Hard to Find

The difficulty comes because, unlike face-to-face conversations, forms have very little context. We can't see the person asking the questions, and often we've never had dealings with them before. We can't hear the tone of their voice, or read their body language. They may even be from a completely different culture or social group. We might not know much about the topic, either. And to top it all off, it's much harder to get clarification through a form than in a face-to-face conversation.

Compared to paper-based forms, web forms are much less forgiving. We all learn the hard way that putting spaces in our phone number may cause an error. Or that the form won't always accept the hyphen in our name.

Of course, to fill out a web form, a person also has to understand and have access to the web, as well as understand written language. You may be surprised to learn that significant proportions of the population struggle with one or both. For example, in the United States, almost a fifth (17.5%) of the adult population understands written English so poorly that they would struggle with even the most basic web form[1]. The figures aren't much different in the United Kingdom (16.4%) or Australia (12.6%).

Some of these adults with poor English literacy would be struggling because English is not their first language. But in our increasingly multicultural countries, people with English as a second language are a core part of our target audience. And speaking English as a second language doesn't necessarily mean low literacy. Think of all the people you know who grew up speaking another language at home (e.g. Mandarin, Spanish or Hindi), but learned English at school. They may even speak, understand and write it better than you or I!

Similarly, 20% of Americans aged 18 or over have neither home broadband nor a smartphone[2]. In both Great Britain[3] and Australia[4], 14% of households don't have access to the internet. In many cases, people in these situations will use

---

[1] http://www.oecd.org/site/piaac/chapter2proficiencyinkeyinformation-processingskillsamongworking-ageadults.htm
[2] http://www.pewinternet.org/2013/08/27/broadband-and-smartphone-adoption-demographics

things like library computers, and will likely have poor or patchy understanding of the digital world. But for other people, you'll need to make sure your web form is not the only way to provide information. (Maybe don't get rid of that paper form altogether.)

As people who work with the web every day, it can be hard for us to imagine having such low digital or language literacy. But this is the reality for many of the users of our forms. As a result, we can't just write what works for us. Instead, we must research our questions with the target audience, just like we would research any user experience we create.

To make the most of our research with users, we want to put our best attempt in front of them. Luckily, scientists have already done some of this research for us, by looking into what happens in people's heads when they are asked, and answer, questions.

What Is a Question?

Before we look at a model for how questions are answered, however, we need to be clear on what exactly a "question" is. Throughout this book, when I talk about a **question**, I mean not just the "asking" part—that is, the *field label*—but also:

- any tips, formatting instructions or other help that accompanies the question (I call this **question-level help**)
- the answer options or spaces (also called the **answer field**).

Let's look at an example. Suppose you're designing an online form for a bank (in fact, we'll do just this in Chapter 4). The following image shows a question to identify existing customers and their rough value to the organization (based on a real form):

---

3. https://www.ons.gov.uk/peoplepopulationandcommunity/householdcharacteristics/homeinternetandsocialmediausage/bulletins/internetaccesshouseholdsandindividuals/2015-08-06

4. http://abs.gov.au/ausstats%5Cabs@.nsf/0/ACC2D18CC958BC7BCA2568A9001393AE?Opendocument

Are you a TD Bank Customer?

(If yes, check all products that apply.)

☐ Checking

☐ Savings

☐ CD or Money Market

☐ Car Loan

☐ Wealth Management

☐ Mortgage

☐ Personal Loan

☐ Home Equity Line of Credit

☐ Overdraft Protection

☐ Insurance

3-3. An example based on a real world banking form, illustrating the different parts of a question

This one question is made up of:

- the label "Are you a TD Bank Customer?"
- the question-level help "(If yes, check all products that apply.)"
- a set of checkboxes as the answer field.

But the form designers could just as easily have chosen to use the approach shown in the image below, which has:

- the label "Which TD Bank products do you currently have?"
- no question-level help
- a different set of checkboxes as the answer field.

TD Bank products you currently have

- ☐ Checking account
- ☐ Savings account
- ☐ Car loan
- ☐ Personal loan
- ☐ Home loan
- ☐ Insurance
- ☐ Something not listed above
- ☐ None

3-4. An alternative wording for our bank question

How do you know which of these two designs—or perhaps yet another alternative—is going to work well, let alone is the best? This is where our model for how people answer questions comes in.

Four-stage Model for Question Answering

Cognitive scientist Roger Tourangeau proposes a four-stage model for how people answer a question:

1. **Comprehension** (understanding words and meaning)
2. **Retrieval** (searching memory, feelings, thoughts and sources)
3. **Judgement** (checking answer suitability, and making adjustments)
4. **Answering** (physically providing the answer).

These stages can happen in a split second, and we're not usually conscious of them. And stages will sometimes be repeated—for example, if the user decides their first answer isn't suitable, and searches for another one.

Once we've come up with a first draft for our questions, we can use each stage from Tourangeau's model to see whether or not users are likely to have difficulties.

Comprehension: Understanding Words and Meaning

At the most foundational level, your questions must be written in such a way that the user can understand them, without strain.

Increasingly, such writing is being referred to as **plain language**. Plain language is writing that works for the target audience, and is as simple and straightforward as possible.

To implement plain language, use:

- shorter, simpler words
- shorter, simpler sentences, each of which expresses just one idea
- the active voice
- words that are familiar to the person filling out the form.

That last point is crucial. In the context of a hospital, a form for a patient may use "heart", whereas a form for a surgeon will probably use "cardiac". If your form is for lawyers, it's fine to use legalese. If it's for technical specialists, it's fine to use their particular jargon. But if it's for the general public, use as little legalese and jargon as possible.

Here's an example. The text in the following image is not plain language:

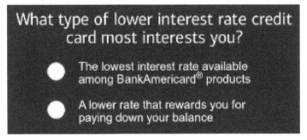

3-5. In this question, neither the label nor the answer fields are written in plain language

Now here's the same question, in plain language:

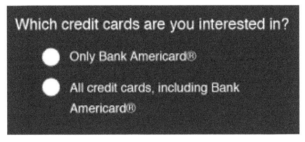

3-6. A plain language re-write of the question in the previous image

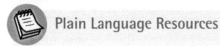

Plain Language Resources

Here are some good places to start learning about plain language:

- An explanation of plain language from the Plain Language Association InterNational (PLAIN)[5]
- "Plain Language: Keys to Success" checklist from the Center for Plain Language[6]
- Free plain English writing tools from the Australian Plain English Foundation[7]
- 4 Syllables' "Resources for web writers"[8] and "Everyday words cheat sheet"[9]
- For those working in government: US Federal Plain English Guidelines[10] plus free tips and tools from PlainLanguage.gov[11]
- And particularly for lawyers, from one lawyer to his peers: "The Pros Know: Plain Language Is Just Good Writing"[12].

And if you'd like to see plain English in action "in the real world", you can read the news in plain English on Voice of America's Learning English website[13].

Don't be fooled: plain language can be challenging to get right. Consider the following question:

Where do you work?

How would you answer it? Perhaps you'd answer according to the organization you work for ("I work for PayPal"). Or maybe the first thing you think of is location ("I work in Austin, mostly, but also sometimes San José"). Or it's possible that a description of your place of work makes the most sense to you ("I work in an office").

[5.] http://plainlanguagenetwork.org/plain-language/what-is-plain-language/#.V4drgI5cRAc

[6.] http://centerforplainlanguage.org/plain-language-checklist/

[7.] https://www.plainenglishfoundation.com/free-writing-tools

[8.] http://4syllables.com.au/resource/

[9.] http://4syllables.com.au/resources/words-cheat-sheet/

[10.] http://www.plainlanguage.gov/howto/guidelines/FederalPLGuidelines/TOC.cfm

[11.] http://www.plainlanguage.gov/howto/index.cfm

[12.] http://www.michbar.org/file/barjournal/article/documents/pdf4article2701.pdf

[13.] http://learningenglish.voanews.com/

There are at least three different ways to answer the question, and probably more. And we can't know how many people will interpret the question in each way. Yet the question seems like plain language: only four words, each word has only one syllable, and the words are all commonly used.

As this example shows, **ambiguity is one of the worst enemies of comprehension**—because we've only succeeded at the comprehension stage if users interpret the question the way we intend them to. We may want users to tell us their location, but as the question is ambiguous, many will tell us about their organization, or describe their place of work.

How do you think you might reword this question to make it less ambiguous? Often the solution is to **use more precise terms**, chosen to suit the information we need to collect. For our work question, we could use "In what location …?", which is more precise than "Where …?". An even more precise wording would be "In which town or city …?" (provided that's what you actually want to know).

But what if the user has more than one job? Or has one job but it involves traveling between a few different places? We need to cater for these situations too, and we can do so by **providing a frame of reference**. Rather than just:

> In which town or city do you work?

we might say:

> In which town or city do you work most often?

(scope determined by frequency), or:

> In the last week, what towns and cities did you work in?

(scope determined by time period). Again, which frame of reference we choose depends on what information we need to collect.

Another important way to improve comprehension is to explore only one concept at a time. This is because the human brain struggles to hold one concept while going through each of the four question answering stages for another. To see this in action, try reading the text in the following image:

If your **family name has changed** or was incorrectly shown on your last notice of assessment, please type your name exactly as shown on your **last** notice of assessment.

Otherwise leave blank and click on **Next** to continue.

Family name

3-7. This question tries to ask about multiple concepts at once

Challenging? You bet. This is because the question is trying to ask about both a change in family name and an incorrectly shown family name, as well as giving complex answering instructions, all at once.

Comprehension is improved if we split the question up into two:

Has your family name changed since your last notice of assessment?

O Yes

O No

Was your family name correct on your last notice of assessment?

O Yes

O No

3-8. Asking one thing at a time makes comprehension much easier

Our redesigned question allows the user to focus on just one concept at a time, go through the four Tourangeau answering stages for that concept, then move on to the next. This makes the experience of filling out the form feel much simpler and easier.

It may also surprise you to learn that even though we're using two questions instead of one—making the form objectively longer—users will feel like the second form is faster to complete. This is because answering the original, multi-concept question requires considerable mental effort. This effort uses up some glucose and makes the user feel just a little bit tired. This in turn makes the experience of filling out the form seem longer. (For the impact of mental effort on perceptions of time see, for example, Zimbardo and Boyd's book *The Time Paradox*[14].)

Note that **it's this *perceived length* that matters**, not the *objective length*. The same principle applies as for rides at Disneyland. Distracting entertainment and lines that wind are just some of the techniques used to create a customer perception that wait times are small enough—so that people will queue, even though the objective wait time is large. As such, you should focus less on how many questions there are on your form, and more on whether the number of questions feels okay to users. But we'll talk more about form length later.

To summarize, comprehension is maximized if you:

1. use the appropriate vocabulary
2. reduce ambiguity, with precise terms and frames of reference
3. explore only one concept per question.

Full Sentence or Brief Prompt?

Before we move on from comprehension, let's look at whether the label should be written as a full sentence or a brief prompt.

Here's an example of a full sentence:

> What is your full name?

and this would be the equivalent brief prompt:

> Full name

Both types of questions can work well.

Brief prompts can be less work for the user, because there are fewer words to process. They may be all that's needed if you're asking familiar questions like "Mailing address" or "Password". But be careful if your form is going to be used internationally: users in other countries may not use the same terms, even if they are ostensibly speaking the same language[15].

---

[14]. http://www.thetimeparadox.com/
[15]. http://www.procopytips.com/american-vs-british-english

Often, however, brief prompts don't contain quite enough information to enable comprehension. For instance, "Name" isn't clear about which parts of the user's name are needed (given name, or family name), and what to do about nicknames, former names, pseudonyms, tribal/indigenous names and so on. Consequently, we may need to use a full sentence like so:

> Your full name, exactly as shown on your driver's license

(For more about collecting names, see "Common Questions" below.)

Full sentences can get tiresome, though:

> What is your daytime phone number? What is your after hours phone number? What is the daytime phone number for your emergency contact? What is the after hours phone number for your emergency contact?

Ugh.

As with any design, the priority should be what makes for the best overall user experience. Be consistent in label style, but not if it hinders comprehension or unnecessarily burdens the user. Many forms mix full sentences and brief prompts, and you probably wouldn't notice unless it was pointed out:

Card number

CCV number

Expiry date

MM ⬍   YYYY ⬍

Please issue a receipt in...

◉ My name   ○ My organisation's name

Please send my receipt via...

◉ Email   ○ Post

3-9. This form includes labels that are both full sentences and brief prompts

2. The address

Postcode

Street Address

☐ Unable to find the address

3. Property occupancy

Do you own the property?   ◉ Yes   ◉ No

Is it your principal place of residence?   ◉ Yes   ◉ No

3-10. Another example of mixed labels

Retrieval: Searching Memory, Feelings, Thoughts and Sources

Replace "Wednesday 22 March" with today's date, and then try answering this question:

Prior to Wednesday 22nd of March, when did you last consume alcohol?

| March | | | | | | |
Mon	Tue	Wed	Thu	Fri	Sat	Sun
27	28	1	2	3	4	5
6	7	8	9	10	11	12
13	14	15	16	17	18	19
20	21	22	23	24	25	26
27	28	29	30	31		

| February | | | | | | |
Mon	Tue	Wed	Thu	Fri	Sat	Sun
30	31	1	2	3	4	5
6	7	8	9	10	11	12
13	14	15	16	17	18	19
20	21	22	23	24	25	26
27	28					

3-11. Question asking about most recent consumption of alcohol

This question is pretty good in terms of comprehension. It uses fairly simple terms, although "drink" would be better than "consume". The frame of reference is clear. Better still, this is a behavioral question, so there's an actual correct answer. But can you provide it?

If you've never had a drink in your life, this will be an easy question! Like many other people, however, you may have found this question difficult to answer accurately (especially if your last drink was more than one or two days ago). This illustrates the role of the second stage in the question answering process: retrieval.

Your form questions must **only ask for information that is available to the user**, either from a secondary source (like printed records) or from their own brain.

If your users will need to get information from a secondary source, such as an electricity bill or another person:

- before the form starts, let them know they'll need this information
- allow time for users to get the information (e.g. have reasonable and extendable time limits, or provide functionality to save and return)
- be clear about exactly what information is needed and where to find it.

Even though it's "on hand", getting good information from the human brain can be more problematic than getting it from a secondary source! Alas, human brains are not nearly as flawless as we may think (heh, see what I did there?). Perhaps you're aware that thoughts and feelings change over time, and depend greatly on context. But did you know that memories also change over time, and depend on context?

In 1992, a cargo plane crashed into an apartment building in Amsterdam, killing 43 people. After the event, there was much media coverage. Ten months later, Dutch psychologists asked a sample of people what they remembered about the crash. To the question, "Did you see the television film of the moment the plane hit the apartment building?", a massive 55% of participants said "yes". Some even recalled details like the angle the plane was at when it hit the building. Yet there was never any footage of the crash!

There's way too much research about memory for us to cover the topic in any depth here. But when it comes to designing questions for forms, there are a few patterns that we can refer to. Importantly, humans tend to remember, and more accurately retrieve:

- memories from conscious experiences, as opposed to sub- or unconscious ones (e.g. accidentally reversing into a tree as opposed to looking in the rear vision mirror during everyday driving)
- memories from events that are emotional (e.g. your wedding day), rather than unemotional (e.g. brushing your teeth two days ago)
- the essentials of a memory (e.g. the organizations you have worked for), rather than the details (e.g. what you did every day at each of those organizations)
- the first and last of things (e.g. the first and last talks at a conference, or your first and last dates)
- memories from more recent experiences (e.g. getting stuck in the rain yesterday) than ones a long time ago (e.g. getting stuck in the rain five and a half years ago)
- things that are highly associated to one another (e.g. remembering what you had for dinner is easier when it's associated with going out for your anniversary, versus a regular weeknight at home)

Satisficing

By now you're hopefully getting a sense of just how much mental effort can be required to answer one question, let alone a series of them on a form. We may not pay much conscious attention to this cognitive burden, but our bodies certainly do. In fact, our brains are always looking for ways to get things done without spending more energy than is necessary.

The technical term for this is **satisficing**. Coined by Herbert Simon in 1957, the word is an amalgam of "satisfy" and "suffice": making do with just enough. Satisficing is something we're all doing all the time, subconsciously. For example, you're satisficing when you scan headings rather than read a whole article, or only look at the first page of Google search results. Rather than spend more time and energy to get something better, we often do only what's needed to get an acceptable outcome.

Forms are no exception. Users satisfice when filling out forms, usually at the comprehension and retrieval stage of question answering. Unless we defend against it through our question wording, this satisficing can lead to errors. These errors often can't be detected through validation, so we need to prevent them altogether.

Remember our change of name question? (It started with "If your family name has changed or was ...", in figure 3-7 above.) Satisficing means that some users will stop reading the question at "changed", believing that they have enough information to answer. But if they stop reading there, they don't have the frame of reference "since your last notice of assessment". Maybe they'll answer "yes" because, for example, their family name changed five years ago when they got married. Such users will answer "yes", duly provide their new family name, and any validation of the answers won't flag that there are issues.

We can defend against such satisficing by **putting frames of reference at the start of the label, rather than the end**. See how this works in the following image:

Since your last notice of assessment, has your family name changed?

O Yes

O No

On your last notice of assessment, was your family name correct?

O Yes

O No

3-12. Change of name question with the frame of reference at the start of the label

Having the frame of reference at the start of the label means it can't be missed. It also primes the memory retrieval process to consider just that period of time.

The next way to defend against satisficing is to **include information needed by all users in the label, not the question-level help**.

Help text suffers from satisficing even more than labels do. If the user (subconsciously) believes they can answer the question without any further assistance, they won't bother reading the question-level help. This is okay as long as the question-level help doesn't contain anything critical to answering the question accurately!

The following image shows a question that appeared on a birth registration form:

Is this the mother's first child?

Include legal adoptions

○ Yes

○ No

3-13. Many users will feel they can answer this question once they've read the label, and not bother to read the question-level help

By putting "Include legal adoptions" into the label itself, we make sure every user is counting the same births:

Including legal adoptions, is this the mother's first child?

○ Yes

○ No

3-14. Putting key information into the start of the label means it won't be missed

Notice it goes at the start of the label, as it's a frame of reference. Notice also how validating the answers wouldn't tell us there's a problem with the question.

Another way to defend against satisficing is a real expert's trick: **turn important instructions into questions**. Satisficing is rampant when it comes to instructions on forms. In fact, it's wise to design your form so that it can be completed without reading any instructions, because that's what most users will do.

But some instructions are critical. You can often make sure they're read by turning them into questions.

Take the following (real) form. Users filling out this form will often read the "Mailing address" heading and jump straight to typing in the address, even if they don't have to:

New Account address

Street

Suburb or town

State

Postcode

Mailing address
You are only required to complete this section if your mailing address differs from the New Account address.

Street

Suburb or town

State

Postcode

3-15. Satisficing means some users will provide their mailing address when they should have left those fields blank

By changing the instruction into a question, this extra effort can be avoided when the account and mailing addresses are the same:

Billing address

Street [   ]

Suburb or town [   ]

State [▼]

Postcode [   ]

Is this also your ○ Yes
shipping address? ○ No

3-16. There's less chance the instruction will be missed if we pose it as a question

You may have seen this trick on an ecommerce form, without realizing what it is. Often such forms ask you whether your billing and shipping addresses are the same. Those of you who are old enough will remember that they weren't always this smart!

Please enter your billing information as shown on your credit card statement. * = Required Field

1 BILLING ADDRESS

Full Name *

Company Name (optional)

Country * AUSTRALIA

Address * Street Address or PO Box

Apartment, suite, unit, building, floor, etc.

Town/City *

State/Territory * - Select -

Postcode *

Phone Number *

Email Address *

☐ Yes, send me upcoming alerts to exclusive CafePress deals and promotions.

2 SHIPPING ADDRESS

◉ Ship to my billing address
○ Ship to a different address
☐ 🎁 This is a gift order.
Check this box to see gift options. Please note that posters are not eligible for gift options.

3-17. Many ecommerce forms have turned the instruction about shipping address into a question

Finally, the most important way to defend against satisficing: don't overburden the user. Fatigue from answering questions is guaranteed to lead to satisficing, and non-completion in general. So keep your questions to a minimum, and make them as easy to answer as possible.

Judgement: Checking Answer Suitability, and Making Adjustments

Users aren't robots, they're people. This means they don't only get fatigued from answering too many questions or ones that are too hard, they also get frustrated, upset and angry. But there's no set rule about when these emotions will be triggered, because it all depends on the context.

You're probably comfortable giving your date of birth on an official taxation form. Would you be just as comfortable if the form were a guest checkout on an ecommerce site? Many people wouldn't be.

When you're asked for your date of birth, you have no trouble comprehending the question, and retrieval usually isn't an issue either. But you'll spend some time thinking about whether or not you want to give that information on this particular form. With the ecommerce site, you may choose not to, if answering is optional. If answering isn't optional, you may choose to use a fake date of birth, to maintain your privacy.

This is the judgement stage of question answering: reviewing whether or not the answer you've retrieved is either right for the situation, or needs modification.

In their book *Forms That Work*[16], Caroline Jarrett and Gerry Gaffney remind us that **a form is a conversation between two parties**. As with a conversation that's face to face or over the phone, things change according to context. Context like:

- social norms and expectations
- culture
- education and literacy levels
- personal experiences and background.

Try to be aware of what's appropriate to ask, and how to ask it, within the particular context of your form. That way, you'll avoid putting users in a situation where they struggle to judge whether to answer, and if so, what answer is appropriate. And if you must ask a question that could raise concerns for users, add some question-level help explaining why the information is needed:

* Do you have a driver's licence?

3-18. Users found this question odd, as it appeared on an application for home electricity. The addition of the question-level help (blue) made users feel comfortable to answer.

---

16. http://www.formsthatwork.com/

The precision we talked about for comprehension also helps with judgement. I was recently asked how often I used my Apple TV to catch up on past shows. Here are the options I was given to choose from:

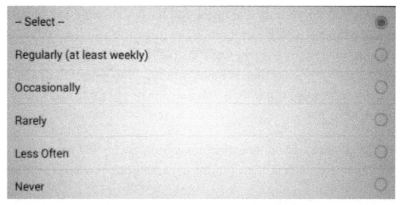

3-19. Ambiguous terms used to describe frequency

They've given a bit of direction as to what counts as "regularly", but what if once a month is what I consider regular? And who knows what would be "less often" than "rarely" but not "never"!

Both the television station and I would benefit from more precise quantifiers. A better approach would be to ask for the number of hours or days per week.

The judgement stage will work better for all parties if you can be precise, especially about the following:

- time frames, weights, dollar values and other quantities
- edge cases
- definitions.

Not only do the words we use in the question influence judgement, so also do the options we provide in the answer field.

The options we provide in the answer field (if any) contribute to the user's interpretation of the question. You can see this in the two examples pictured below, which ask our earlier question about work. The label is the same in both questions, but the answer fields are different. Clearly the two questions will yield different answers from each other, as well as from a question where the answer field is a blank text box:

3-20. Same question, different answer options

Answering: Physically Providing the Answer

Phew! So far, we've worked hard to make sure that:

- our question can be effortlessly comprehended
- users can accurately retrieve the information from their memory or somewhere else
- we've been precise and clear to simplify judgement.

The users are now ready to actually *answer* the question. Why would we hobble them at this last hurdle? Because it's scarily easy to do!

Ever been faced with a form like this?

Recipient Name :	
AddressLine 1 * :	
AddressLine 2 :	
AddressLine 3 :	
AddressLine 4 :	
AddressLine 5 :	
AddressLine 6 :	
City/District/Locale/Locality* :	
State/Province :	
Postal Code/Zip Code* :	
Country :	Australia

3-21. This form has multiple problems with the way it collects an address

Some folks will be overwhelmed at the number of address fields, and not know how to divide their address amongst them. Others will see "AddressLine 1" and started typing in their address, only to find they've put the city in "AddressLine 2". And what if I live in Hong Kong or the United Arab Emirates, where there are no postal or zip codes?

It's surprisingly common for forms to make it difficult for a user to provide the right answer. Here's another example. Perhaps you, like me, work from home. But you can choose only one!

Will this order be shipped to a business or residence?

ⓒ   Residence   ⓒ   Business

3-22. This form has multiple problems with the way it collects an address

Or maybe there's just no answer for you to choose at all (despite the question being mandatory):

3-23. This form made me choose the domain for my email address from a dropdown, but the dropdown was empty

Then there's the beloved options provided for you when you'd much rather type in your answer:

✓
No Street Number
1A
1B
1
2A
2B
2C
2D
2E
2
3-5
3-7
3B
3R
3
4-6
4
5-5A
5-7
5A
5B

3-24. Forcing the user to choose from a list may help keep the database neat, but it's a nightmare for users

I could go on, but I think these examples are enough to show the importance of answer field design.

Open Versus Closed

For each question on your form, the first design choice you have to make is whether to let users type in their answer (called an **open** question) or have them choose an answer from options you provide (called a **closed** question).

From a user experience point of view, **closed questions are often ideal**, because they:

- help the user interpret the question
- minimize the user's workload
- minimize errors.

However, you should only make your question closed if you can reasonably provide—*and actually know*—the right set of answer options. Guessing options will only lead to problems for the user, increased errors and reduced data quality. This is mostly because it's very hard to walk in the shoes of all your users, so you're likely to leave out options that are needed, and make mistakes with the options you do put in.

Of course, if you have a large enough number of participants, user research is a great way to gain information about what the options should be. If you can't do the research yourself, see if someone else already has.

Characteristics of Usable Closed Answer Fields

There are six characteristics of usable closed answer fields.

Characteristic 1: they are **appropriate**. The options presented:

- cover the main answers users will want to give
- come from reputable, relevant and timely sources
- are not too detailed and not too broad
- are reviewed and updated on a regular basis.

How do you describe yourself?*

3-25. The only thing this list of descriptions is appropriate for is the trash

Characteristic 2: they are **complete**. There must be an option for each and every user, including "other", "don't know", "none of the above" and "not applicable", as appropriate:

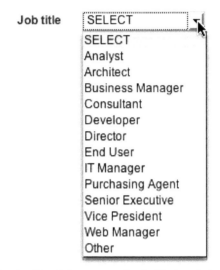

3-26. This question about job title should really have a an option for "Designer", given it's from a form about Adobe design products

With continuous scales such as periods of time, try to make sure the "ends" are open:

When was the last time you, yourself purchased each of the following.

(Please answer for each)

	Within the last week	Within the last 2-3 weeks	Within the past month	One month to 3 months ago	3 to 6 months ago	More than 6 months ago	Within the past 12 months	Never
Mouth-wash	⊙	○	○	○	○	○	○	○

3-27. The top end of this scale isn't open, so there's no way to answer "More than 12 months ago"

You should also ensure that no one falls into a gap between periods:

1   *How long have you been an NGV Member (formerly known as the Gallery Society?)

⚪ 12 months or under

⚪ 1-2 years

⚪ 3-4 years

⚪ 5-10 years

⚪ 10+ years

3-28. If the user has been a member for two and a half years, they fall through the gap between these options, and might not know how to answer

Characteristic 3: the options provided are **mutually exclusive** (they don't overlap):

S1. Are you the owner, general manager, or a key decision-maker of this business?

◉ Business owner

○ General manager but not a business owner

○ Key decision maker

| | Other (specify)

3-29. Much like the residence or business question, the options here are not mutually exclusive

Characteristic 4: the options are **self-explanatory**, so that users have no trouble comprehending them:

Time of Day
☑ ANY
☐ INT   ☐ MAT
☐ MOR   ☐ EVE

3-30. Only experienced theater-goers would have even a clue what these options mean

Characteristic 5: the options are appropriately **sorted**, or presented in a suitable order, and grouped into categories, if appropriate:

Amount: *

✓	Please select...
	£40.00
	£50.00
	£80.00
	£100.00
	£30.00
	£60.00
	£120.00
	£150.00
	£55.00
	£65.00
	£130.00

3-31. Thanks to the crazy order of options in this dropdown, many users won't notice amounts that might be what they want

 ## Alphabetical Order

Only put options in alphabetical order if:

- there's really only one term used for each option
- users know those terms well, and
- there's no other more suitable or natural order.

For instance, it would make sense to put US states in alphabetical order (Alabama, Alaska, Arizona, Arkansas ...), but it would be unwise to put satisfaction ratings in alphabetical order (Agree, Disagree, Neither agree nor disagree, Strongly agree, Strongly disagree).

As such, alphabetical order should almost be your last choice, when you've determined that no other more logical order exists.

Characteristic 6: the options are **unbiased**. They don't skew in one particular direction, as here:

	extremely strongly	very strongly	strongly	only slightly	no preference
How strongly do you prefer Lufthansa rather than any other airline?	○	○	○	○	○

3-32. Bad luck if you don't prefer Lufthansa, or actively avoid them

Punctuation at the End of the Label

People often ask me: "Should I use a question mark at the end of my question?"

Stop for a moment and ask yourself whether, given what you've read so far, the question answering process is likely to be influenced by a question mark (or colon, or something else, or no end punctuation at all). Which of the four stages—of comprehension, retrieval, judgement and answering—would punctuation relate to?

Punctuation affects comprehension. (Did you get it right?) In prose writing, punctuation helps convey the tone and pauses. In forms, however, we expect questions, so punctuation is often less critical. The visual design—that is, the placement of text next to fields—also provides a cue that it's a question label. So in the scheme of things, **it matters little whether you use a question mark (?), a colon (:), something else, or nothing at the end of a label**.

Whatever you choose, try to be consistent. If your labels are mostly full sentences, you might want to use question marks. If your labels are mostly brief prompts, colons may be more appropriate. Both cases would often be fine without any punctuation at the end of the label at all. But as with the label style, we want to be consistent unless and until it compromises the user experience.

This may include consistency with your organization's style guides. Perhaps your organization takes a minimalist approach to punctuation, in which case you might want to leave it off the end of your labels. Or maybe your organization insists on question marks at the end of every question, regardless of whether or not it appears in a form.

Question-level Help

Up until now, we've been implicitly focusing on the question label, but everything we've discussed applies equally to **question-level help**. Question-level help is an integral part of the comprehension, retrieval, judgement and answering stages. Just imagine trying to answer the question "Password" correctly the first time without question-level help:

Password

3-33. Who knows what type of password will meet this site's validation rules?

Here's the same field with question-level help:

Password

Must be 6 or more characters and contain at least 1 number

3-34. The question-level help tells the user what kind of data will be acceptable, preventing an error

Here's another example of question-level help:

Year of Publication or Creation*

▼

If approximate, provide earliest date to begin search.

3-35. This question-level help tells the user what to do if they can't provide an exact date, although it could be written more clearly

This question-level help even includes a picture—the easiest way to show where something is:

The CSC is the last 3 digits found on the back of your credit card. The CSC (Credit card Security Code) is not part of your credit card number.

CSC:

3-36. An example of question-level help around the CSC question on a credit card form (also known as CCV or CVV).

Notice how, in all the examples above, the question-level help is presented right there, as part of the question, not buried in a separate "help" file. This improves the user experience by making the form more usable, accessible, touch-friendly and faster (all part of our criteria for <u>"One Design to Rule Them All"</u> in Chapter 1). Moreover, you've seen just how much work the user has to do to answer questions. Why would we add to their burden by tucking away information that will help?

 Rotten Repetition

There's something even worse than not providing question-level help when it's needed, and that's repeating the label verbatim:

Your first name*   (* required)

> Your first name

Last name at graduation*

> Last name at graduation

Current last name

> Current last name

Email address*

> Email address

3-37. In this form, *every single label* is repeated as question-level help

Do not do this!

Not every question has to have question-level help. It's another example of our mantra from Chapter 2:

> Start with nothing. Then only add what's needed to communicate with the user.

In other words, only add question-level help if it adds something important to the question.

Deciding What Questions to Ask

Information Need

So now you know how to ask a question well—and you're getting a sense of how user research can be so valuable!

But what questions are you even going to ask? Before you start moulding the wording for your questions, you need to decide what information it is that you need.

The second habit in Stephen Covey's world famous *The 7 Habits of Highly Effective People*[17] is:

> Begin with the end in mind.

This is a great mantra for form design.

To decide which questions you need, imagine your form has already been filled out, and examine how the resulting data is going to be used. Into what business processes will it input? What decisions will it inform?

Be specific and concrete. This is not about how data might be used at some unknown future point, but what exactly is needed right now. **Every additional question on a form reduces the completion rate and data quality, while also increasing the rate of errors**. So we must have justification for each and every question. Also, because humans are averse to loss, you'll find it very difficult to remove questions later, even if the resulting data isn't being used. It's much easier to add questions that are missing.

Data Quality

There's one type of question that comes from a legitimate information need, but should never be asked: one that can only yield poor-quality data. An example is a question like the one pictured below:

[17.] https://www.stephencovey.com/7habits/7habits.php

How Did You Find Out About Us?

3-38. A typical marketing question, attempting to identify the source of a lead

As you can appreciate from reading about "Retrieval" and "Answering", "How did you hear about us" questions generate notoriously inaccurate data. Not only are users unlikely to accurately remember something so banal and unimportant (to them), many just choose any answer (a good example of <u>satisficing</u>), or don't answer at all, just to get past the question.

Here's another example:

Pacific Magazines Pty Ltd would like to occasionally contact you with offers and information. But if you prefer not to receive them please tick here:
☐ by post ☐ by phone
Please tick here if you would like to receive relevant messages by SMS:
☐ from us ☐ from our partners
Sometimes our partners have relevant offers. But if you don't want to hear from them please tick here:
☐ by post ☐ by phone

3-39. An attempt to garner more mailing list entries through deceptive wording

This is an example of a **dark pattern**: a deliberate attempt to trick the user through design. Any short-term gain will be undone by the long-term pain of user dissatisfaction and broken trust. Avoid dark patterns like the plague.

The four-stage model tells us what other types of questions will yield poor-quality data: anything that pushes the user too far in terms of comprehension, retrieval, judgement or answering. It can be as simple as asking users to remember something they can't, like the question about their last drink of alcohol from "Retrieval", or putting shoe sizes in a strange order:

SIZE ⌄

☐ 1	☐ 10
☐ 11	☐ 12
☐ 13	☐ 2
☐ 2½	☐ 3
☐ 31	☐ 35
☐ 35.5	☐ 36
☐ 36 - UK 3	☐ 36.5
☐ 37	☐ 37 - UK 4
☐ 37.5	☐ 38
☐ 38 - UK 5	☐ 38.5

3-40. You can bet some wrong-sized shoes were ordered thanks to this filter

Poor-quality data is worse than no data at all, because it can:

- steer you in the wrong direction (e.g. high levels of satisfaction stemming from a question that only has positive answer options)
- undermine the organization (e.g. deceive users into giving an answer that's the opposite of what they meant).

The upshot is, it doesn't matter how badly someone wants it, **questions can only be asked if they can be answered accurately**.

How Long Is Too Long?

Another common query I receive is: "How long can the form be?"

Common sense would suggest that the longer the form, the lower the completion rate. There certainly are plenty of case studies supporting the idea that shorter forms work better than longer forms. Marketo found that having only three questions instead of five lifted the conversion rate by 25% and also reduced the cost per lead by 25%[18]. Formisimo achieved a 16% increase in sign-up conversions< by removing one field and providing a facility to show the password[19]. Imaginary Landscape reduced their Contact Us form from 11 questions down to only four, and achieved a 160% increase in conversions![20]

An article by Micah Shull on the Marketing Experiments blog[21] gives a great analogy:

> The easiest way to improve the functionality of a website is to remove things. Think of your website as a lush tropical jungle in Central America and your online explorers are trying to reach an ancient Aztec temple. The temple holds all the value, and is the reason people are willing to explore the jungle. The rainforest can be an amazing experience, but the thick understory and sprawling root systems can become obstacles on the path to the temple.

18. http://www.marketingexperiments.com/blog/internet-marketing-strategy/lead-generation-testing-form-field-length-reduces-cost-per-lead-by-10-66.html
19. http://www.formisimo.com/blog/case-study-small-changes-lead-to-a-55-increase-in-conversions/
20. https://www.imagescape.com/blog/2008/06/10/new-study-compares-short-and-long-contact-us/
21. http://www.marketingexperiments.com/blog/analytics-testing/testing-value-copy-and-friction.html

Micah is talking about general website design here, but the analogy works just as well in reference to forms. Your forms are the jungle, and the temple is whatever goods or services the form is a gateway to.

There's just one problem: it's not as simple as "fewer questions = better form", because **subjective length matters more than objective length**. Sometimes, the user experience is improved by more questions (and more words in labels and question-level help, and more answer options). The change of name question shown above in figure 3-7 and redesigned in figure 3-8 is a good illustration of this.

When discussing comprehension, we've seen how a single complex question is harder to answer than multiple simple questions, which makes the form experience feel longer. Therefore, if you focus too much on making your form *objectively* shorter—e.g. minimizing the number of questions or screens—you may actually make it *feel* longer.

The subjective perception of length is also influenced by the nature of the questions within the context of use. If you're asking me to sign up for a service I'm not even sure I'll use, even just "username" and "password" may be two questions too many. But if I'm doing something serious, like my income taxes, I may be very willing to answer 11 desktop screenfuls of questions. In fact, I recently conducted research on a form about family violence protection orders, which confirmed just that.

In the end, it all comes down to fitness for purpose. For forms, there's no "right" length. You need to find out whether the length of your particular form matches (or surpasses) the expectations of its particular users in its particular context. If not, you've got some editing to do.

Common Questions

You can now see that sometimes, writing good questions is quite a bit of work! Wouldn't it be great if we didn't have to do all that work every time, from scratch, with every new form? After all, surely some questions come up again and again.

There are some questions that are common to many forms, such as:

- Title
- Name
- Address
- Email
- Phone
- Date of birth
- Sex and gender
- Credit card details.

Unfortunately, it seems every system and organization wants a slightly different version of even these common questions. One web form needs a postal address, the other asks for a billing address, and a third wants a shipping address. One site may limit passwords to eight characters, while another may insist on a *minimum* of eight characters!

This means there's no one right way to ask each of the common questions listed above. But don't despair! There are some good defaults, as well as traps to look out for, which I can share with you here.

Title

The following image shows a typical title field:

3-41. Ah, the beloved title field

Do everything you can *not* to have a title question on your form. Why? Because whatever design you use, it won't work for some of your users.

Many users won't want to choose a title. Some of those that do will inevitably find their title isn't listed, or they can't find it in the ludicrously long list that includes "Vice Admiral" and "Honorable Lady". On top of this, a title can expose some highly personal information about your users, like sex, gender or marital status.

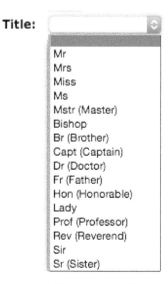

3-42. What, no Corporal?

"But how will we know how to refer to the user in correspondence?" I hear you say. Simple: ask the user. The following image shows a good way to do this. After all, users may not like to be addressed by their title anyway:

Your Profile
please enter your details

Full name

What should we call you? (If we send you mail, for example?)

3-43. Ask users how they would like to be addressed

If you *must* have a title field, try to make it optional, and let the user just type it in:

Title (optional) [   ]

3-44. The best way to ask for title, if you have to

 Don't Use Title as a Proxy

It can be tempting to use title to decide on a person's sex, gender or marital status. Don't. There isn't a consistent, stable correlation between title and these other characteristics (see, for example, >"When 'Mistress' Meant 'Mrs.' and 'Miss' Meant 'Prostitute'"[22]. For instance, someone who is married may like to use "Miss". Another person may use "Mr" but identify as male transitioning to female (see also "Sex and Gender" below). And good luck working out the sex, gender or marital status of a Doctor or a Professor!

Name

The structure of people's names differs greatly between cultures, languages, location and background. Some people have a single name (e.g. Stilgherrian or Demirel) or a very short name (e.g. Wu Yi). Some people have very long names with multiple parts (e.g. Abu Karim Muhammad al-Jamil ibn Nidal ibn Abdulaziz al-Filistini, or Bhaktavatsalam Bhayakridbhayanashanachar). And there are people with every variant in between.

Many "special" characters are also entirely normal in people's names. This includes apostrophes (e.g. O'Donnell or D'Arcy), diacritics (e.g. Renée or Günther) and hyphens (e.g. Jean-Paul or Freeman-Wallace). Spaces, a mix of upper and lower case, non-Latin characters—the list of "unusual" elements that are completely accurate in names goes on.

To cater for this, your best default is to collect someone's name by using:

- a single text answer field
- a precise label.

[22.] https://newrepublic.com/article/119432/history-female-titles-mistress-miss-mrs-or-ms

Here's an example of this approach:

Full name

3-45. The best default for collecting someone's name

If you must break the name up into parts, try to use "Given name(s)" (instead of "First name", "Middle name" etc.), and "Family name" (instead of "Surname", "Last name" etc.):

* Given name(s)

* Family name

3-46. Collecting a person's name in parts

This is because name orders can vary: some people's first name is their given name, but other people's first name is their family name.

If the name the user enters has to match some other source, tell them so in the label. Credit card is a familiar example of this:

Credit Card Information

Name on Card:

3-47. Being specific about the name that's needed

Of course, this advice applies to cultures that are primarily English speaking. If your form is going to be used a lot by other cultures, you may need to do more research.

 ## Resources About Names

If you want to read more about the complexity of names, a good starting point is:

- "The name riddle"[23]
- "Personal names around the world"[24]
- "Falsehoods Programmers Believe About Names"[25].

Address

"Name" is one of those questions that seems crazily simple, but is actually really hard to get right. "Address" is another example—again thanks to variability around the world.

First of all, the label. **Never just ask for "address"**; be specific about the type of address you need (e.g. home, work, postal, shipping or billing).

Next, as with names, be sure to allow "special characters" like apostrophes and hyphens.

Now the hard bit. If you can, a good default is to collect addresses:

- via a single text answer field
- with (accessible) auto-suggest
- through relevant and frequently-updated databases.

In other words, unless your context suggests otherwise, the best default way to collect an address is the way Google Maps does it:

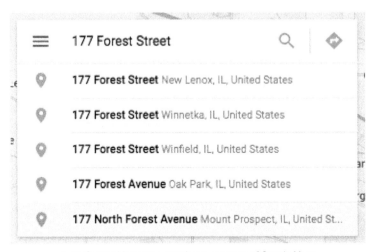

3-48. Great address user experience, courtesy of Google Maps

---

23. http://www.formulate.com.au/blog/the-name-riddle

24. https://www.w3.org/International/questions/qa-personal-names

25. https://www.kalzumeus.com/2010/06/17/falsehoods-programmers-believe-about-names/

If this approach isn't possible, you'll need to find out which geographical locations your question must cover (e.g. one country, multiple countries, or all international addresses) and tailor your approach accordingly. A fantastic source of information—including international postal address formats—is the GRC Data Intelligence website[26] from Graham Rhind.

Email

Email addresses are, thankfully, much simpler than other types of address. Use a single text answer field with the label "Email address":

Email Address *

3-49. Collecting an email address is simple

Here are some other things to remember:

- Make the email address question optional if some users may legitimately not have email addresses.
- Include question-level help, describing why the email address is being collected, if users need to know this (see figure 3-50 below).
- Make sure the field accepts a large number of characters, as email addresses can be very long.
- Avoid setting rules other than that there be one character before the "@" and one character after, as the international specification for email addresses is too complex for more detailed validation rules[27].
- Use the HTML5 `type="email"` input attribute to bring the right keyboard up for mobile users. (See "Touch Device Smarts" in Chapter 5.)

[26.] http://graham-rhind.com/
[27.] http://haacked.com/archive/2007/08/21/i-knew-how-to-validate-an-email-address-until-i.aspx/

Email *

We'll send your order confirmation to this address

3-50. If users should know, explain why you need their email address

Phone

Phone number collection is a bit of a mix between address and email. These are some important things to remember:

- You need to specify which number you want (e.g. home, work, daytime, after hours, landline, mobile or cell).
- A single text answer field is a good default. (See figure 3-51 below.)
- Special characters like hyphens, dashes, periods (full stops), parentheses and spaces should be accepted.
- Collecting international phone numbers is challenging.
- Use the HTML5 `type="tel"` input attribute to bring the right keyboard up for mobile users. (See "Touch Device Smarts" in Chapter 5.)

My mobile phone number is: [   ] (Optional)

3-51. A good default for collecting a phone number

Date of Birth

You should avoid collecting date of birth, as it's quite personal information, often used to prove identity. Consider if it would suit your purposes just to collect a person's age, perhaps in a range:

14. My age group is:

◯ Under 20

◯ 20 - 29

◯ 30 - 39

◯ 40 -49

◯ 50 - 59

◯ 60 plus

3-52. Sometimes all that's needed is age, not actual date of birth

Or maybe all you need is confirmation that the user is old enough:

☐ I am over 13 years of age.

3-53. Another alternative to asking for date of birth

If you do need date of birth, the fastest, most accurate and most accessible way for a user to enter it (because of its familiarity) is by typing it out.

You can use:

- a single field (shown in figure 3-54), ideally with the `type="date"` input attribute, which brings up the in-built date picker on mobile (see <u>"Touch Device Smarts"</u> in Chapter 5), or
- separate fields (as shown in figure 3-55).

Date of birth

Example: 15/7/1988

3-54. Single field for collecting date of birth

Date of birth

DD   MM   YY

3-55. Separate fields for collecting date of birth

For the pros and cons of the two approaches, see <u>"What to Use Instead of (or in Addition to) a Date Picker"</u> in Chapter 4 (which also covers the challenges of international date picking).

Sex and Gender

For many people, sex and gender are sensitive and highly personal subjects. They're also two concepts that are rarely dealt with correctly in forms.

Sex is the biological—but not binary—distinction between male and female. "Biological" can mean anatomical (e.g. breasts or a penis), hormonal (e.g. level of estrogen) or chromosomal (e.g. X, XY or XXY).

Gender is how a person identifies (psychologically) or expresses themselves.

Someone's gender may or may not make reference to their biological sex. For example, a person with female genitalia may feel like, and identify as, a man. Another person may identify as "genderqueer", signifying that they see themselves outside the binary constructs of male and female (which are sometimes called "cis male" and "cis female").

The range of terms used to describe gender is wide and culturally specific. Examples include transexual, androgyne, nongender, third gender, questioning, female-to-male (FTM) and male-to-female (MTF).

You can see how personal and sensitive sex and gender are, and thus recognize the corresponding care we have to give these questions on our forms. It can also be illegal to ask about sex and gender. As such, **you shouldn't ask about sex and gender unless you really have to**. If you do have to ask, make sure you're asking about the right thing, in the right way, and are allowed to do so.

For sex, this is a good default:

Sex

○ Female

○ Intersex

○ Male

○ Unspecified

○ None of the above

3-56. Recommended sex question

Notice how, aside from "none of the above" (which obviously has to go last), the options are in alphabetical order, to minimize any perception of discrimination.

For gender, a single text answer field is likely to be the best approach:

3-57. Rather than try to categorize people's gender, let them describe it themselves

This caters for all users, especially as there's no single list of genders accepted by everyone everywhere.

Both of these approaches to collecting sex or gender information should be optional, or include a "prefer not to say" option, if at all possible.

Credit Card Details

Perhaps because they're so common, people are always trying new approaches to collecting credit card details. Feel free to attempt something fancy with flipping card faces or some other pretty layout, like the design in figure 3-58—but only if you have research confirming usability:

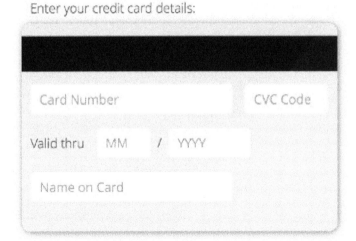

3-58. Fancy credit card question design

Alternatively, you can go with the design like this, which just works:

3-59. Recommended credit card question design

Note that the payment type is worked out computationally, based on the initial digits of the card number. At first, the payment type icons serve to show what cards are accepted. Once the user has entered enough digits for the card type to be determined, it's highlighted:

Card number	**5446**
Payment type	
Expiry date	mm yy
	/
CVV	
What is this?	

3-60. Users should never have to choose a credit card payment type, as this can be determined from the card number

This design has many benefits:

- it works for all credit cards, no matter their layout
- it only asks the minimum number of questions needed to process a credit card
- it asks questions in the same broad order as the card
- it collects data in the same format as the card
- it doesn't require any special formatting by the user
- it's lightweight and fast

Display Payment Options

It should be ecommerce 101 to inform users up front of the type of payment methods you'll accept. All too often, forms and sites don't provide this information until the very last step of payment—despite the availability of payment methods being known to influence purchasing behavior!

This is especially true for cards that aren't always accepted—such as American Express (in the United States, United Kingdom and Australia), Diners Club (United Kingdom), Alipay (China) and JCB (Japan). Users who want to pay with these cards will be greatly reassured if you tell them that they can, as early in the payment process as possible.

We've done this in the real world for years:

3-61. Physical stores often display the payment methods they accept in their windows or displays (image credit: PT Money)

Online, the equivalent would be in the header of your website:

3-62. Payment methods shown in the site header

Or in the footer:

3-63. Payment methods shown in the site footer

And whenever you reach a major purchase decision point:

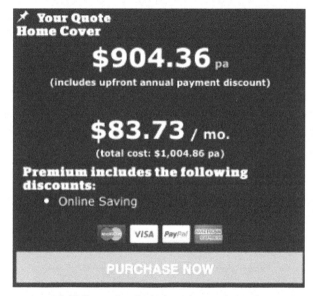

3-64. Payment methods shown in a quote reveal

And, of course, as a more proximate reminder at the point of payment:

3-65. Payment methods shown next to payment fields

Other Words in Forms

While the text we place directly on each form field is the most crucial to get right, there are other places we use text in our forms. How we word this other content matters too.

Headings

In all written texts, headings are like signposts. They indicate content and direction. But do forms need them? The answer is sometimes yes, sometimes no.

Form Title

There's one heading every form should have: the **form title**—or the name of the form. The form title needs to appear on each and every screen of the form. It tells users where they are, especially after distraction or interruptions (many forms are not completed in one sitting).

Ideally, form titles should:

- be brief (five words or fewer)
- be unique (within your organization)
- be descriptive.

And they shouldn't:

- contain redundant words like "form", "online" or "web"
- contain words like "a", "the" and "for" (the title is a handle, not a complete summary).

Here are some examples of effective form titles:

- Personal Loan Application
- Motorcycle Insurance Quick Quote
- Log in to Emirates Skyawards
- Book Travel
- Search Cars
- Enroll to Vote
- Australian Passport Renewal Application

Section Headings

Section headings can help users by flagging a change of topic. In shorter forms, though, section headings can create more work for the user, without much benefit. They can also make the form seem longer and more burdensome.

An example is the registration form in figure 3-66. The headings here are not especially informative and make the form look bigger. Plus, the topic changes as much between questions as it does between sections. So the headings here don't really help.

3-66. The section headings "Details" and "E-News" don't add much to this form

A good approach is to start without any section headings, and only add them if they deliver real value to the user. But be careful: users often decide whether or not a section applies to them based on the heading. If you do include them, section headings must be accurate and easy to understand.

Questions Posing as Section Headings

Avoid what the form in figure 3-67 below does: conflate questions with section headings. As we've said before, users often focus on questions and don't read other text on the form unless they absolutely have to. Thus, if your questions are posed as headings, users often won't see them:

3-67. The middle section heading in this form is actually the question

Step Headings

Some forms are divided into multiple steps. These steps may be presented over multiple screens:

3-68. In this mobile form, we're currently on the "Verify identity" step)

Or the separate steps may be presented in an accordion layout:

Secure Checkout

Step 1: Account Details	Creating an account	Modify »
Step 2: Billing & Account Details	Jessica Enders, PO Box 24121, Melbourne, Victoria, Austra...	Modify »
Step 3: Shipping Details	Jessica Enders, PO Box 24121, Melbourne, Victoria, Austra...	Modify »
Step 4: Shipping Method		

Please choose the shipping method for your order:

     ◯ Free Shipping $0.00

[Continue]

| Step 5: Order Confirmation | | |

3-69. Accordion form with clear step headings

In multi-step forms, the purpose of the step heading parallels that of the form title: communicating place. Thus, multi-step forms should always have a step heading. Also, like form titles, step headings should be brief, unique and descriptive, avoiding redundant words like "information" and "details".

You can use the word "Step" in your step heading as per figure 3-69 but you don't have to (as figure 3-68 shows). You can also choose whether or not to number the steps. If there's a high number of steps, you might not want to number them, as it may call attention to the form's length.

By the way, we'll discuss how to format your headings in the "Typography" section in Chapter 4.

Button Labels

Buttons are a small but critical part of a form's design. The visual design (see Chapter 4) and the text label are what determine whether the user can actually move forward through the form!

Like headings, button labels should be brief and descriptive, such that users have no trouble deciding whether or not to use them. Furthermore, button labels should always contain an action (hence the term "call to action"[28] in the language of marketing and conversion optimization).

Here are some good button labels:

[28.] http://www.hongkiat.com/blog/call-to-action-buttons-guidelines-best-practices-and-examples/

- Add to cart
- Add to wish list
- Apply now
- Back
- Buy now
- Cancel
- Checkout
- Continue
- Create account
- Donate
- Download
- Finish
- Get quote
- Log in
- Next
- Pay
- Place order
- Previous
- Save
- Search
- Send request
- Sign up

Try to avoid "Submit" if you can. Although it's more familiar to users than it was ten years ago, it's still jargon: it doesn't really say what submitting *means*, and is only used where a proper label hasn't been specified.

Also make sure you use the right label at the right time. Recently, I was filling out a form with the button labels shown in figure 3-71. I thought "Done" meant I'd finished filling out the form. Imagine my surprise when another screen of questions loaded! I'll never understand why they chose "Done" instead of "Next".

3-70. "Done" is a good label for the final step of a form, but not when there are more questions to answer

Messages

At least once in every form, and often many times more, we need to communicate a message to the user. These messages may indicate status, highlight important information, or prompt the user to act.

Continuing our analogy of a conversation, we want all messages to users to be timely, clear and polite. This is especially important with error messages. After all, it may be the designers or developers who made a mistake, not the user.

In fact, after question wording, the wording in error messages is one of the most crucial components of the form. Let's have a closer look at the wording of error messages.

Error Messages

Every error message should do three things, all with a polite and non-accusatory tone:

1. convey that an error has occurred
2. be clear about exactly what and where the error is
3. tell the user what they need to know to correct or move past the error.

This doesn't have to mean a lot of words, as this image shows:

Enter your email

Please enter your email.

3-71. This simple error message does everything an error message should

Remember to use plain language, which we talked about earlier. This means, for instance, you don't say "Required field" but rather "This question must be answered":

| *Guest Last Name | | Required field |

3-72. You might not realize it, but people that don't work in our industry often have no idea what "Required field" means

Actually, you want to be as specific as possible (for example, "Your email address is missing an '@'", rather than "You must provide a valid answer for this question"). This will enhance accessibility as well as usability.

It's also crucial that you're clear about what needs fixing, so the user can move forward:

| Phone number | (02) 6116 8765 | Please enter a valid Australian phone number |

3-73. This is actually a valid Australian phone number, so presumably the system is grumpy about not receiving it in a particular format. The problem might be the parentheses, the spaces, or both, but the message doesn't say!

And you should never blame the user or be rude:

Name
| S | Is your name really that short?? |

3-74. This error message is mean!

The validation behind error messages, as well as details on how these and other messages should be presented, can be found in Chapter 5 (Flow).

General Instructions

Most of the instructions on your form should appear at the question level, so that they're "just in time":

But there may be instructions that apply at a section, step or form level.

Research consistently shows many users don't read such general instructions, unless they are really struggling with something and think it might help. So as much as you can, design the form so that the general instructions won't be a barrier to completion (but also aren't just waffling). And remember the trick about turning instructions into questions.

The following image presents a good illustration of a form with general instructions that are largely useless, except for a key point (in bold), which should be turned into a question:

Open And Close An Account

Thank you for choosing Horizon Power as your energy services provider. We are committed to providing our customers with a reliable, high-quality service.

Please complete the form below in order to close your current Horizon Power account, and open a new account at your new address. If any additional details are required we will contact you.

If you are a registered Life Support Customer, please phone us on 1800 267 926 so one of our Customer Service Representatives may assist with your needs.

* Indicates a mandatory field.

```
┌─ Personal Details ──────────────────────────────
│  Title *
```

3-75. The general instructions at the top of this form can be removed, provided the last sentence is turned into a question

Contrast the image above with the one below, where the general instruction is useful, yet brief, and not necessary for successful completion:

Join ASOS

Signing up with social is quicker than email. No extra passwords to remember - no brain fail.

3-76. This is an effective general instruction

Here's another good example of a general instruction:

Who's traveling?
Traveler names must match government-issued
photo ID exactly.

First name *

Middle name

Last name *

3-77. The text beginning "Traveler names" is an effective general instruction

As always, start without any general instructions and only add them in if they're really needed to communicate something to the user. Writing your general instructions should follow the same general principles as for labels and question-level help.

Yours or Mine?

Personalization has been big on the web for a while now. With forms, this trend has led to the injection of possessive pronouns such as "my" or "your" into form questions, headings and other text. Is this good for the user experience? And which is better: "my" or "your"?

Start Without Pronouns

In forms, the possessive pronoun can get in the way really quickly:

Your First Name*:

Your Last Name*:

Your Email Address*

Your Country*:

Your Country *   ▼

3-78. Even with just the small number of fields shown here, the "your" is likely to get very annoying

In many cases, you're better off without the pronouns. "My" or "your" are redundant, and add to the user's mental workload.

Where Pronouns Can Be Helpful

If the user has logged in to fill out the form, "my" can work well. "My dashboard" or "My saved forms" may fit this category. "My" can get tricky really fast, though, if the form needs to "talk" to the user. If "my" is already taken, what can we use to represent the voice of the organization or form? This is where "your" often works better.

Referring to More Than Two Parties

Sometimes, in a single form, we need to distinguish between more than two different parties. An example would be a complaint form being submitted to an independent investigator. Here, we need to be able to identify:

- the user who's making the complaint

the person or organization the complaint is about

the person or organization who'll investigate the complaint.

In this situation, we may want to use "your" for the user, because the form is talking *to* the user in the voice *of* the investigator. Descriptive terms can then be used to refer to the other parties.

Is this making your brain hurt? It might help to imagine the same information being collected face to face: the investigator would use "your" to refer to the user making the complaint.

Words That Work

As we saw right at the start of this chapter, users can overcome poor layout but not poor wording, so you've got to design your wording well. This design must always be focused on your target audience, who may have varying degrees of language or computer literacy.

This has been a long but important chapter, so let's end by recapping what we've covered.

We saw that Tourangeau's four-step model for question answering can serve as a useful checklist:

1. **Comprehension** (understanding words and meaning)
2. **Retrieval** (searching memory, feelings, thoughts and sources)
3. **Judgement** (checking answer suitability, and making adjustments)
4. **Answering** (physically providing the answer).

Don't forget to apply the model to all parts of the question:

labels

question-level help

answer fields that work for the user.

For comprehension, the main pointers are to:

use the appropriate vocabulary

- reduce ambiguity, with precise terms and frames of reference
- explore only one concept per question.

For each of these, use full sentences or brief prompts, with or without punctuation at the end of the label—whichever works best.

Retrieval can come from three sources:

- the user
- someone else
- something else.

But the peculiarities of memory, and the subconscious practice of satisficing, mean none of these is infallible.

Context affects all stages of question answering, but especially judgement. You can minimize the burden here by:

- thinking of the form as a conversation
- only asking what's appropriate
- being precise
- using the answer fields to help communicate to the user.

To enable users to actually answer, you need to choose carefully between open and closed questions. For closed questions, make sure the options are:

- appropriate
- complete
- mutually exclusive
- self-explanatory
- sorted
- unbiased.

Knowing some of the ways to design good questions, we moved on to deciding which questions to ask. Here the important considerations are:

- collect only what you need
- don't collect poor-quality data
- ensure that the form length matches or surpasses a user's expectations.

We looked at some good default designs for common questions, such as name and credit card fields.

We then moved on to other words in forms—headings, button labels and general instructions. You now know that every form must have a title, but section and step headings are only needed in some cases. Button labels should be named with the same care as question labels. And general instructions should be avoided if at all possible.

Finally, we looked at possessive pronouns like "my" and "your", which can appear in many parts of a form. As with words in general, an effective approach is to start without these pronouns, only adding them in if there's a real need. "Your" may work better than "my" if the form/organization needs to have a voice.

So now you have a solid toolkit of tips for your form's words. In the next chapter, we'll see where these words—as well as all the other pixels!—should be placed.

Chapter 4

Layout

Forms have many elements in addition to words, like actual fields and buttons. In this chapter, we'll look at the best way to visually design these elements—what they should look like, and where they should go. For simplicity, we'll refer to this as **layout**.

A Mantra: It's All about Balance

There are *lots* of forms out there that look absolutely fantastic. Unfortunately, this is how many people judge forms: by how they look. But as we saw in Chapter 3, a form that can't be filled in is no use to anyone, no matter how attractive it is.

The best forms strike a balance between user experience and aesthetics.

Another way to put this is that we want to lay out our forms so they can be filled out quickly, easily, and accurately, while still looking good. Thus, our focus will be on the aspects of layout that impact user experience. But for the most part, that also results in a visually appealing form.

For Realz

To learn about designing a form, there's nothing like actually designing a form! So through this chapter, we're going to design an application form for an Australian business bank account.

I've chosen a form for opening a business bank account—rather than a personal one—because it will allow us to discuss all the key field types. The form has an Australian focus because it's where I live and what I know. The principles apply just as well to forms from any country that is primarily English-speaking (and therefore reads from top to bottom, left to right).

The fields in the form are labeled as follows:

- Business trading name
- Australian Business Number (a unique identifier for Australian businesses, known by the abbreviation ABN)
- Given name
- Family name
- Date of birth
- Email address
- Country where head office is located
- Total number of employees
- Social networking sites used for marketing activities
- Can we send you information about special offers and new products?

Abbreviations

Abbreviations such as "ABN" are best avoided, because they're often jargon or technical terms that users may not understand. (For more on jargon and technical terms, see "Comprehension" in Chapter 3). All existing Australian business holders will know what an ABN is, because they have to have one to operate. But people new to Australian business may not know the abbreviation, especially if they are attempting to open an Australian business bank account before registering their business.

We have to decide which group the design will be optimized for. This decision will depend not only on numbers (e.g. which group of users is greater—existing or new businesses?), but also on factors like our organizational priorities. For instance, new businesses may be the minority of users, but may also be the focus for customer growth. This is why there are very few form questions for which one particular wording can be prescribed as best practice. Context can change everything.

In this case, we're going to take a middle ground and use the abbreviation, but explain it via question-level help.

Choose Your Field Types

Most questions can use one of three main answer field types:

- checkboxes (users can choose none, one or many options)
- radio buttons (users can choose none or one option)
- text boxes (users type in their answers).

These types are great because:

- users are familiar with them, even if they've mostly filled out forms on paper, not the web
- they work on all screen sizes, including mobile
- they're built into the HTML specification
- they're accessible out of the box
- they're simple to use in design and development.

We could design our example form with just these three types, no problems at all:

4-1. We can design a workable form with only text boxes, checkboxes and radio buttons

All other field types are "enhancements" on the main three. For instance:

- a dropdown is just a set of *radio buttons* collapsed into a smaller space
- a segmented control is also just a set of radio buttons collapsed into a smaller space
- a switch is two radio buttons collapsed into a smaller space
- a multi-select dropdown is a set of *checkboxes* collapsed into a smaller space
- a date picker is an alternative to three text boxes
- a one-handled slider is an alternative to a single text box, or a set of radio buttons
- a stepper is also an alternative to a single text box, or a set of radio buttons
- a two-handled slider is an alternative to *two* text boxes, or *two* sets of radio buttons.

While our example form could be done with just the three field types, it's much more common to see some of these "enhancements" being used. For instance:

- Country where head office is located: **dropdown**
- Date of birth: **date picker**

- Total number of employees: **slider**

Business Bank Account Application form mockup:

BUSINESS BANK ACCOUNT APPLICATION   ☺ Enders Bank

Business trading name* [_____]

ABN* [_____] You must have an Australian Business Number (ABN) to apply for an Enders business

Given name* [_____]

Family name* [_____]

Date of birth* 📅

Email address* [_____]

Country where head office is located* [Choose a country ▾]

Total number of employees* |——————●————————| Include full time, part time, casual and contract employees.
1   More than 200

Social networking sites used for marketing activities* ☐ Facebook ☐ Twitter ☐ Pinterest ☐ LinkedIn ☐ Vine ☐ Insta

Can we send you information about special offers and new products?* ☑ You can opt-out at any time.

[Apply] [Cancel]   *Must be answered

4-2. Using some "enhancements" to our answer field types

These "enhancements" must be good, right?

Problems with Using "Enhancements" to Answer Field Types

"Enhancements" is in quotes for good reason. In many cases, the alternatives to the three main field types can actually make the experience *worse* for users, not to mention making development and maintenance more challenging.

Issues with Dropdowns

Dropdowns have many problems, including the following:

- Many users don't know how to use them, as they have no real-world or paper form equivalent (unlike checkboxes and radio buttons).
- Many users don't know how to navigate them with the keyboard, causing the user to switch between keyboard and mouse.
- The options are initially hidden.

Often not all options can be seen at one time.

Some options are placed a long way away (e.g. United States and United Kingdom near the end of a country list).

They require at least twice as much interaction compared with checkboxes and radio buttons (because of the click to open).

They're not easy to use on touch devices, where the desired option can be particularly tricky to navigate to and select.

In other words:

The devil is in the dropdown.

And you can quote me.

What to Use Instead of a Dropdown

If you can, **use radio buttons** (choose one option) **or checkboxes** (choose multiple options):

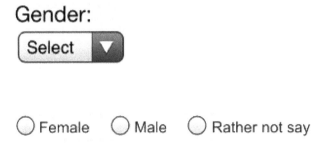

4-3. Sex being collected via a dropdown (top) versus radio buttons (bottom). Note that the label should actually be "Sex", instead of "Gender"—see "Common Questions" in Chapter 3 for more information.

The dropdown in our example form is for the question about head office country. Here's how (the start of) it would look as radio buttons:

Country where head office is located*   ○ Afghanistan
                                        ○ Åland Islands
                                        ○ Albania
                                        ○ Algeria
                                        ○ American Samoa
                                        ○ Andorra
                                        ○ Angola

4-4. Radio buttons for head office country

When coded properly, the answer field *label* is clickable, not just the actual radio button or checkbox. To support touch, you can also change the presentation of the options so they have a large visible touch area around them:

Country where head office is located*   ○ Afghanistan

                                        ○ Åland Islands

                                        ○ Albania

                                        ○ Algeria

                                        ○ American Samoa

                                        ○ Andorra

                                        ○ Angola

4-5. Radio buttons with visible touch area

Sometimes radio buttons are even made to look like *actual* buttons:

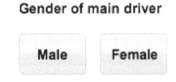

4-6. Radio buttons with visible touch area

Long Lists of Options

As you can see in Figure 4-3 above, radio buttons and checkboxes make good replacements for dropdowns *when there aren't too many options for the user to choose from*. Our head office country question does have too many options, and will use up a lot of space on the screen. After all, we're only showing part way through the letter A in figures 4-4 and 4-5 above. If we showed all the countries of the world, there'd be no pages left for the rest of this book!

The situation gets even worse if we think about filling out this form on the smallest screen size—that of a mobile device. A long list of country radio buttons is going to go over several screenfuls:

4-7. Country radio buttons on a mobile

We could move the options to a different screen, so at least the form doesn't look too long initially. On larger screens, this is how it would work:

Enders Bank – Business Bank Account Application

BUSINESS BANK ACCOUNT APPLICATION

Business trading name*

ABN*   You must have an Australian Business Number (ABN) to apply for an Enders business

Given name*

Family name*

Date of birth*

Email address*

Country where head office is located* Choose a country

Total number of employees* |————●————| Include full time, part time, casual and contract employees.
1   More than 200

Social networking sites used for marketing activities* ☐ Facebook   ☐ Twitter   ☐ Pinterest   ☐ LinkedIn   ☐ Vine

Can we send you information about special offers and new products?* ☑ You can opt-out at any time.

Apply   Cancel   *Must be answered

4-8. Moving selection to another screen. First we show a button to initiate that screen.

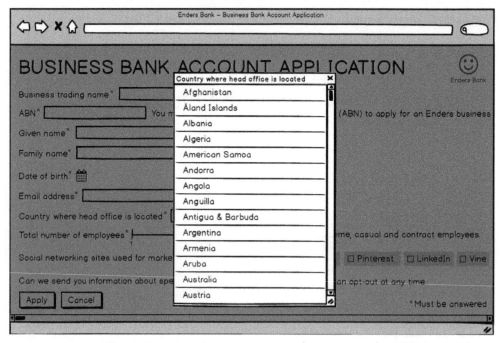

4-9. When the button is used, the alternative screen (or modal window) is loaded

And on mobile:

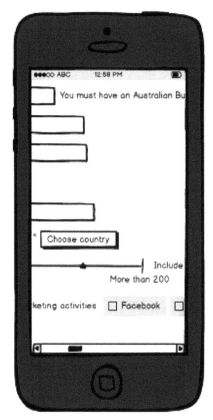

4-10. Button to initiate country selection

4-11. New, separate screen for country selection, which could slide in and then slide out again when selection is made

But this really just pushes the problem somewhere else.

The better solution is to use a text box with auto-suggest. This approach works if users are likely to know what the options are (that is, they don't need to see them to know how to answer). People know what country their business is in, so they don't need to see the list of countries to be able to answer:

Country where head office is located [   ]

Country where head office is located [uni   ]

Reunion

Tunisia

United Arab Emirates

United Kingdom

United States of America

United States Virgin Islands

4-12. Text box with auto-suggest

Now with this example, I've picked probably the most ubiquitous long list of options on the web: country. And you may have noticed I'm recommending *against* using a dropdown, which has been somewhat of a norm until now. But for good reason.

Currently unpublished data by the UK Government Digital Service (GDS) shows that users often struggle to make a selection when there are more than about 20 options. Usability testing I've conducted shows that a text box with auto-suggest can eliminate this issue.

On mobile, where we have to be particularly careful with our interactions, the text box with auto-suggest also has about the same workload as a dropdown. One tap to put focus in the text box (same as the dropdown); then one or two taps on the keyboard—in comparison to one or two scrolls—to select the country (in our example).

Implementing Country Text Box with Auto-suggest

The way you implement country text box with auto-suggest can influence its usability. A good explanation of the main features can be found in "Redesigning The Country Selector"on Smashing Magazine[1]. The resulting plugin can be found on the >Baymard Institute's sitespan class="fn">http://baymard.com/labs/country-selector.

But remember, a text box with auto-suggest is an alternative to all long lists, not just country selection. Here's another example, this time a long list of radio buttons for selecting medical speciality. The radio buttons took up seven mobile screenfuls, even with the keyboard hidden!

Speciality

☐ Acute Medicine

☐ Allergy

☐ Anaesthetics

☐ Anatomy

☐ Audiological Medicine

☐ Breast Surgery

☐ Cardio-Thoracic Surgery

☐ Cardiology

☐ Career Management

☐ Chemical Pathology

4-13. First screenful of a question collecting medical speciality via a long list of radio buttons

---

[1] https://www.smashingmagazine.com/2011/11/redesigning-the-country-selector/

Things work much better with a text box plus auto-suggest:

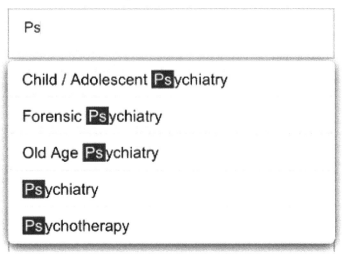

4-14. The same question with a text box plus auto-suggest for the answer field

If users *won't* know the options without seeing them, you might have to use a dropdown, unless you have the resources to make a custom widget. The UK government digital service created just such a widget for their listing of "Competition and Markets Authority cases":

4-15. Custom widget to allow multiple selections from a long list of options

Because of the special wording used to categorize cases, the types had to be shown to users. A list of checkboxes would have taken up too much space, yet the designers didn't want to use a multi-select dropdown. In came the custom widget.

As the developers of this custom widget will tell you[2], it was not easy to build. Because of the large number of browser and operating system combinations, custom widgets take a lot of time to code and test. So they really should be your least preferred option.

Segmented Controls and Switches

On to our next "enhancements".

A **segmented control** presents options in a visual group, from which the user must choose one:

4-16. The user must select from three options

Segmented controls take up less room than a series of radio buttons, by putting the options beside each other and removing the actual radio buttons.

For options with short labels, like those in figure 4-16 above, the segmented control works well. But as soon as you have longer labels, you run into problems.

It can also be tricky to design a segmented control to be clear which option is selected. This is particularly so when there are only two options:

4-17. Which is the selected option: the blue or the white one?

---

2. http://jqueryuk.com/2015/videos.php?s=bin-your-

Some may argue that if there are only two options, you should be using a switch rather than a segmented control:

4-18. A switch between off and on. Bonus points if you can tell whether the switch is currently on or off

Even with switches, though, it takes some effort to see and understand which option is selected and which is not, especially if there are no other switches in the vicinity for comparison. And really, they are better for communicating whether something is on or off rather than a choice between two options. This is, after all, what switches were designed for.

If these issues weren't enough to put you off, on the web both segmented controls and switches are custom widgets; they aren't part of the HTML5 standard. As we saw when discussing dropdowns, custom widgets come with many usability, accessibility and cost disadvantages. It's unlikely they'll be worth your while.

Last but not least, these are very *new* widgets in the world of the web. In fact, I've never seen a web form with a switch in it. As such, many users won't know how they work, and may not even realize they're being presented with options from which to make a choice. If your users have to think, as Steve Krug would put it[3], you've created a poor user experience.

What to Use Instead of a Segmented Control or Switch

Stick with good ol' radio buttons.

Don't forget, by putting shading around each option, you help users know they don't have to click right on the tiny little circle:

---

[3]. http://sensible.com/dmmt.html

Will you care for the child with a partner?

◯ Yes

◯ No

4-19. Radio buttons with clickable/tappable area shaded

Date Pickers

To include a date picker in your form, your developers are probably going to get one from whatever framework or library they're using. Unfortunately, the vast majority of date pickers are badly designed, hard to use or inaccessible.

Here's a typical date picker we might use to ask for the date on which a business started to trade:

‹		November 2015				›
Su	Mo	Tu	We	Th	Fr	Sa
25	26	27	28	29	30	31
1	2	3	4	5	6	7
8	9	10	11	12	13	14
15	16	17	18	19	20	21
22	23	24	25	26	27	28
29	30	1	2	3	4	5

4-20. This picker doesn't provide good options for dates a long way from now

The arrows either side of "November 2015" take you forward and back by a single month. Now imagine if the business started trading on 23 April 1975!

Here's another example. The date picker in the image below was designed for use on a mobile. I bet users would be sick of tapping by the time they got to 23 April 1975:

4-21. On this form, the user can type their date of birth or use the (well-designed) date picker

For these reasons, **date pickers should always be an optional way to input dates, never the only way**:

Date of birth

4-22. On this form, the user can type their date of birth or use the (well-designed) date picker

In particular, never ask people to input a *date of birth* via *only* a date picker, or three *dropdowns*:

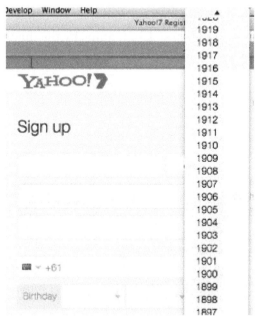

4-23. Three dropdowns make for a lot of work to enter a date of birth

These are laborious ways to enter information that users can type faster. And if you don't know what else is wrong about dropdowns and date pickers, re-read the last few pages!

International Date Picking

You may already know that in the United States, dates are written in a different sequence from how they're written elsewhere, including the United Kingdom and Australia. In the United States, the month is given before the day, whereas the United Kingdom and Australia write the day before the month. For instance, "5/7/1998" would mean 7 May 1988 in the United States, but 5 July 1988 in the United Kingdom and Australia.

To prevent confusion, be explicit about which parts of the date go in which box, and use letters (e.g. "DD") instead of an example date (e.g. "5").

But there's *another* gotcha about international dates: in the United States, it's the custom to consider *Sunday* as the start of the week, whereas in the United Kingdom and Australia, *Monday* is considered as the start of the week. This means if you're using a date picker from a US-derived framework or library, it may well structure the calendar with *Sunday* as the leftmost column of dates.

If your users are from the United Kingdom and Australia, they may navigate subconsciously to the leftmost column and choose a date, assuming it to be a Monday. This happens often, and has cost at least one organization millions of dollars in refunds!

If you do include an (optional) date picker, try to:

- default to an appropriate date
- ensure users can select a month or year different from the default, without having to "arrow" their way back through each month of the calendar
- display months with words (e.g. "Jan") rather than numbers (e.g. "1"), to be clear for international users
- disable dates that make no sense (e.g. dates in the future, when providing a date of birth)
- ensure users can still just type their date into text boxes.

What to Use Instead of (or in Addition to) a Date Picker

Give users a text box for each part of the date you need to collect (day, month or year):

4-24. Overall, the best way to collect date of birth is via three text boxes

If you're really clever, you can provide a single text box for the entire date, but only if you can handle a variety of inputs (e.g. "23/5/1975" or 23rd April '75):

Date of birth

Example: 5/7/1988

4-25. A single text box for collecting date

Or you can write (accessible) code to restrict entries to the required format:

4-26. A single text box with required format

The single text box has the advantage of few clicks/taps, especially important for touch devices.

One Text Box or Many?

The additional work for users is an important reason to avoid using multiple text boxes where a single text box will do. The most common example of this is credit card number: a single text box for the whole number allows the user to type, uninterrupted, and with the smallest number of clicks and taps. It also allows the user to enter the number in whatever way makes sense for them, including chunked or not chunked, with or without spaces etc. After all, you can always reformat the number into a specific pattern after they've entered it.

If you *must* use multiple text boxes, **don't automatically move the cursor from one box to the next**. Doing so is inconsistent with other fields on the form. It also means the interface is doing something without the user's prompting, yet the user should always be in control. Finally, doing this will cause errors for users who are watching the keyboard (and not the screen) as they type.

Regardless of how many text boxes you use to collect a date, don't forget to:

- include question-level help explaining the format you're looking for (e.g. DD/MM/YY)
- code your text boxes with HTML5's `type="date"` attribute, so that users on mobile will be presented with the in-built date pickers for their operating system.

Putting this all together, the image below shows how date of birth should look on our example form:

4-27. The ideal way for us to collect date of birth

Sliders and Steppers

Ah, sliders. Fun in restaurants, painful in forms.

Sliders are a complicated way to do something that's actually really simple—such as provide a single number:

4-28. A slider to provide a single number: age

Sliders are sometimes used to collect a pair of numbers:

4-29. A slider to provide a price range

The reasoning behind sliders—to visually show people that there's a spectrum along which they can make a selection—isn't necessarily bad. But in too many cases, sliders are fiddly to operate, and they make it nearly impossible for the user to provide exactly the answer they want:

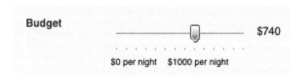

4-30. Setting a budget like $235 is a real challenge with this slider

And that's even *if* the user has small fingers and excellent fine motor skills.

I think many designers include sliders in their web forms to try to make them "fun". But it's no fun wrestling with a widget that's standing between you and the end of filling out a form.

 Sliders in HTML5

Sliders have been included in the HTML standard for the first time with HTML5. In the standard, they're set with `type="range"` on an input. However, the standards-based slider is missing some key visual components[4]. Not included are the value of the current selection, and the end points of the range.

A **stepper** is a control that allows the user to increase or decrease a number by one:

4-31. The plus and minus buttons allow the user to change the number of rooms up or down by one

Steppers provide a minor improvement in user experience—e.g. one less click or tap—when a number needs to be changed by only small amounts. But as a custom control, they're likely to create a disproportionate amount of work relative to the benefit they provide. For reasons described in "Defaults" in Chapter 5, you also need to be careful about providing defaults, like the number of rooms in figure 4-31 above.

[4.] https://dev.opera.com/articles/new-form-features-in-html5/#input-range

 Spinners

Equivalent in functionality to the stepper is the so-called **spinner**, included on an input in HTML5 with `type="number"`:

How many people would you like to invite?

4-32. The arrows inside the right end of the text field appear when the input field includes type="number"

Here, the up and down arrows have the same effect as the plus and minus buttons in the stepper.

Spinners can be good for small numbers (e.g. number of rooms), but they're *terrible* for big ones (e.g. Australian post codes, which are four digit numbers like 2550). It's possible to hide the spinners[5], so your poor users don't think they have to up arrow 2,549 times.

But inputs with `type="number"` get complicated quickly—way beyond the scope of this book. (See, for example, "Numeric Inputs — A Comparison of Browser Defaults" on CSS-Tricks[6] or "Phone: numeric keyboard for text input" on Stack Overflow[7]. If you think you want to use this part of HTML5, definitely have a chat about it with your developer(s).

What to Use Instead of a Slider or Stepper

A single text box will usually work just fine:

---

[5] http://stackoverflow.com/questions/3790935/can-i-hide-the-html5-number-input-s-spin-box

[6] https://css-tricks.com/numeric-inputs-a-comparison-of-browser-defaults/

[7] http://stackoverflow.com/questions/6178556/phone-numeric-keyboard-for-text-input/31619311

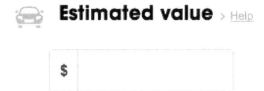

4-33. A single text box is a much simpler way to collect a value than a slider

With our example form, we actually started with a text box. It turns out to have been a solid solution!

Total number of employees [   ] Include full time, part time, casual and contract employees.

4-34. A text box to collect the number of employees

If the range of options is small, you could also use one or two sets of radio buttons (for a single or pair of values, respectively), or a set of checkboxes:

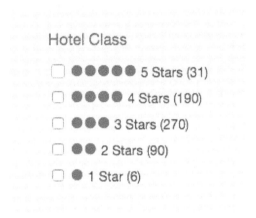

4-35. Checkboxes are much simpler than a slider

Therefore, if we don't need the exact number of employees for our bank account form, but just an indication of size, we could use radio buttons:

Total number of employees ○ 1-49   Include full time, part time, casual and contract employees.

                            ○ 50-199

                            ○ 200 or more

4-36. Radio buttons to collect the number of employees

Single Checkboxes

There's just one last thing to mention with respect to field types. Notice the single checkbox for the last question on our form (marketing consent):

Can we send you information about special offers and new products? * ☑ You can opt-out at any time.

4-37. Marketing consent question with a single checkbox

It's common to use a single checkbox for such questions. But single checkboxes require users to do a little bit of mental calculation, to link the checked/unchecked state to the wording of the question. Things get even more complicated if the question is stated in the negative:

To unsubscribe from the following newsletter communication, please review your selection and click "submit".

☑ **Microsoft Lumia**
Get the latest Microsoft Lumia information, tips and promotional offers from Microsoft.

4-38. A single checkbox with a negatively worded question

It should be clear by now how much we want to avoid any unnecessary cognitive effort. So ideally, you should replace all single checkboxes with yes/no radio buttons. They are just that bit more explicit and direct:

Can we send you information about special offers and new products? *   ○ Yes   You can opt-out at any time.
                                                                     ○ No

4-39. Marketing consent question with yes/no radio buttons

With this final change, our form now has the right ingredients:

Enders Bank – Business Bank Account Application

BUSINESS BANK ACCOUNT APPLICATION

Enders Bank

Business trading name*

ABN*   You must have an Australian Business Number (ABN) to apply for an Enders business

Given name*

Family name*

Date of birth*   DD   MM   YYYY   📅

Email address*

Country where head office is located*

Total number of employees*   O 1-49   Include full time, part time, casual and contract employees.
                             O 50-199
                             O 200 or more

Social networking sites used for marketing activities*   ☐ Facebook   ☐ Twitter   ☐ Pinterest   ☐ LinkedIn   ☐ Vine

Can we send you information about special offers and new products?*   O Yes   You can opt-out at any time.
                                                                      O No

Apply   Cancel   *Must be answered

4-40. Our bank account application with our ideal answer field types

But it doesn't look particularly nice—especially on mobile:

4-41. Our bank account application as it currently looks on mobile

We'll start to consider what we can do about that.

Alignment

You and a friend are each driving to a restaurant for dinner. Both of your routes go down a highway with two lanes. The highways are the same length. On your route, all the slow cars are doing the right thing and sticking to one lane, so you can whizz past in the other. On your friend's route, the slow cars are scattered across both lanes of the highway, so she has to weave in and out. Which one of you will get to the restaurant first?

Vertical Path to Completion

A straight, unobstructed route is fastest for driving, and also for form filling. So your next step is to vertically line up all your form fields, as well as the main button on the page (called the **primary action button**):

4-42. Answer fields and the primary action button are vertically aligned

Now you've created a straight, unobstructed, vertical path to completion. Not only have you made it faster for your form to be filled out, it looks neater and simpler too. (We'll talk about the distance between some fields and their labels shortly.)

Don't Put Questions Beside Each Other

Because a vertical path to completion makes a form longer, you may be tempted to squeeze some questions next to each other:

Pay with a Credit Card

Cardholder Name

Card Number   Security Code

Expiration Date

Country

Australia

House Number or Name

Street

City   Postal Code

CONTRIBUTE ▶

4-43. In this form, the Security Code and Postal Code questions have been put beside other questions

This is a bad idea, for the following reasons:

- It interrupts the smooth flow through the form (like a broken down car in your fast lane).
- Users will often not see the question on the right-hand side, because it's outside the focus of their vision (this is only about nine characters wide).
- It prevents the form from working seamlessly on both large and small screens. (More on this shortly.)

Also, as you may recall from <u>Chapter 3</u>, for users it's the *perceived* length of the form, not the actual length, that matters. The vertical path to completion makes form filling not only objectively faster, but it makes it *feel* fast.

Aligning Answer Fields

One way you can sometimes save space, however, is with answer fields. Look at the answer fields for the marketing consent question:

Can we send you information about special offers and new products?*   O Yes   You can opt-out at any time.
O No

4-44. Marketing consent question, with vertical answer fields

Whenever the answer fields are small, we can put them horizontally. (For this purpose we define "small" as three or fewer options, all with short labels.) The form will still work for touch, and on small screens. Marketing consent is just such a question:

Can we send you information about special offers and new products?*   O Yes O No   You can opt-out at any time.

4-45. Marketing consent question, with horizontal answer fields

In fact, date of birth is also a question with small answer fields. You may not have realized we've already put them on one line:

4-46. The date of birth question has three small answer fields

But remember: you can only put answer fields beside each other if they're small. Otherwise, the design won't work in some cases. Social networking, for instance, has quite a large number of answer options. If we try to put them horizontally, they'll go off the edge—especially on mobile—and invoke the dreaded horizontal scrollbar:

4-47. If we position a long set of answer fields horizontally, we're likely to conjure the horizontal scrollbar, even on larger screens

4-48. If our answer fields aren't small, it's even more likely we'll cause the horizontal scrollbar to appear on mobile

Assuming we can't build a custom widget, it's better to leave these as a single vertical list:

4-49. Larger sets of radio buttons or checkboxes should be vertically aligned

4-50. Vertical alignment of sets of radio buttons or checkboxes works on mobile too

Label Placement

There's a problem with the mobile view of our form, which you may have noticed from some of the illustrations above. On a small screen, when the focus is in a text box, the corresponding label isn't visible, just like this example:

4-51. Labels on the left are seen initially but disappear when the user starts to fill in the form

We could avoid this problem by always putting the labels above the fields. But this creates a new problem: the form becomes a lot longer visually.

Here's how it would look on a large screen:

Enders Bank – Business Bank Account Application

BUSINESS BANK ACCOUNT APPLICATION

☺ Enders Bank

Business trading name*

ABN*

You must have an Australian Business Number (ABN) to apply for an Enders business bank

Given name*

Family name*

Date of birth*

DD MM YYYY 📅

Email address*

Country where head office is located*

Total number of employees*

○ 1-49   Include full time, part time, casual and contract employ

○ 50-199

○ 200 or more

Social networking sites used for marketing activities

☐ Facebook

☐ Twitter

☐ Pinterest

☐ LinkedIn

☐ Vine

☐ Instagram

☐ Tumblr

☐ Google+

Can we send you information about special offers and new products?*

○ Yes   ○ No   You can opt-out at any time.

[Apply] [Cancel]

*Must be answered

4-52. Forms are longer when labels are positioned above fields

What you need to do is code the form to be *responsive*. **When the screen is larger, labels should go to the left of fields; when the screen is smaller, labels should go above fields.** That way, we make use of the space we have on larger screens, while ensuring the form can also be filled out on smaller screens.

If we code our example form to be responsive, this is how it would look on a mobile:

4-53. On mobile, labels are positioned above the fields so they're visible when you need them

This is how it would look on a larger screen:

Enders Bank – Business Bank Account Application

BUSINESS BANK ACCOUNT APPLICATION

☺
Enders Bank

Business trading name*

ABN* You must have an Australian Business N

Given name*

Family name*

Date of birth* DD MM YYYY

Email address*

Country where head office is located*

Total number of employees* O 1-49 Include full time, part time, casual and contract employ

O 50-199

O 200 or more

Social networking sites used for marketing activities ☐ Facebook

☐ Twitter

☐ Pinterest

☐ LinkedIn

☐ Vine

☐ Instagram

☐ Tumblr

☐ Google+

Can we send you information about special offers and new products?* O Yes O No You can opt-out at any time.

Apply Cancel *Must be answered

4-54. On larger screens, labels are positioned to the left of fields so the form doesn't look unnecessarily long

Here's a real-world example of responsive form labels—first the larger screen version of the form, then the smaller screen:

Have you attempted to contact the trader in an attempt to solve your problem?	○ Yes ○ No
Have you lodged this complaint with the Victorian Civil and Administrative Tribunal (VCAT) or a court?	○ Yes ○ No
Are you a trader making a complaint against another trader?	○ Yes ○ No
Is your dispute regarding a private sale?	○ Yes ○ No
Have you lodged this complaint with another organisation, such as an ombudsman?	○ Yes ○ No

4-55. On larger screens, labels are to the left of fields, so the form appears nice and short

Have you attempted to contact the trader in an attempt to solve your problem?

Yes

No

Have you lodged this complaint with the Victorian Civil and Administrative Tribunal (VCAT) or a court?

Yes

No

Are you a trader making a complaint against another trader?

Yes

No

Is your dispute regarding a private sale?

Yes

No

Have you lodged this complaint with another organisation, such as an ombudsman?

Yes

No

4-56. On smaller screens, labels are above fields, so they're always in view

What about *That* Study?

One of the most popular articles on the UXMatters website, and quoted in Luke Wroblewski's book and articles, is an eyetracking study by Matteo Penzo[8]. This study is frequently used as evidence that labels should *never* go to the left of fields, but always above.

[8.] http://www.uxmatters.com/mt/archives/2006/07/label-placement-in-forms.php

The problem is, you should never base design decisions on a single study, especially one with an unknown methodology, and very minor differences in results! Instead, you need to weigh up all the different pros and cons, based on theory and observations from user research. When you do this, it's clear that—on a large screen—the benefits of having labels to the left of the fields outweigh the costs. It's worth a very minor increase in eye movement to have a form that's half as long.

Avoiding the Gutter

In addition to what's been said already, there are two ways you can increase the usability of your form when you have labels to the left of your fields. These techniques are important to prevent a big "gutter" appearing between the labels and their answer fields:

4-57. For many questions on our example form, the label is far away from the corresponding answer fields

These gaps can make it hard for the user to associate labels with their answer fields.

If the labels are mostly short, you can set them flush right, so they're next to the fields:

4-58. Labels set flush right

If the labels are mostly longer, they'll get hard to read if they're flush right. In this case, set them flush left (like normal text) but add zebra striping to your form:

4-59. Zebra striping behind labels set flush left

Zebra striping is the faint shading you see behind every second question. It helps the eye connect the label to the field (as demonstrated by a study I conducted a while back[9], and its follow up[10]).

[9.] http://alistapart.com/article/zebrastripingdoesithelp
[10.] http://alistapart.com/article/zebrastripingmoredataforthecase

(If you want to read more about label placement, I wrote >a detailed article on the SitePoint website[11], and provided some commentary on my own website[12] too.)

Button Alignment

Single-step Forms

If you have just one primary action, line it up with your fields for fast completion. This is what we've done with our example form:

[11.] https://www.sitepoint.com/definitive-guide-form-label-positioning/
[12.] http://www.formulate.com.au/blog/eyetracking-research-and-form-design

4-60. Left edge of the primary action button lines up with the left edge of the fields

Multi-step Forms

If your form goes over multiple steps, you'll need to provide buttons for the user to move between steps. One option is to put the next button in line with the fields, consistent with our single-step forms:

When and where were you born?

Date of birth (dd/mm/yyyy)

Town/City/Suburb of birth

Country of birth

State of birth (if born in Australia)

Are you of Aboriginal or Torres Strait Islander descent? (Optional)

Next   Back   Save draft and exit   Cancel

4-61. Next is our primary action, so it's vertically aligned with the fields

Another option is to put the next button to the right and the previous button to the left (for an English-speaking audience):

◀ Back   NEXT ▶

4-62. English speakers typically think of right as forward and left as backward, so we can align our buttons this way

Both approaches have been shown to work well, but it can depend on the context. If you're not sure which is right for your form, run some usability tests with your target audience.

(You can also put multi-step forms into an accordion, but accordions have a number of usability issues so are best avoided.)

Buttons on Mobile

On small screens, you may want to design your buttons to be responsive, so that they:

- are stacked, with the primary action on top
- take up the full width of the screen, except for a little bit of whitespace on either side (so that they're still clearly buttons).

4-63. Coding our form to be responsive to screen size, we can make sure buttons still work well on mobile

By now our form is looking really good, and is highly usable to boot. But there are further improvements we can make.

Spacing

We can subtly communicate with the user through a few tweaks of spacing.

Proximity

Human beings see things that are close to each other as being related. Conversely, things that are not related usually have some space between them.

These principles tell us to put the parts of a question—label, question-level help and answer fields—close together. Our form is pretty good for this so far, but let's just move the labels a bit to the right, so they're closer to their fields:

4-64. Flush right labels should be close to their fields

On the other hand, there needs to be some distance between each question:

BUSINESS BANK ACCOUNT APPLICATION

☺
Enders Bank

Business trading name* [ ]

ABN* [ ] You must have an Australian Business N

Given name* [ ]

Family name* [ ]

Date of birth* [DD] [MM] [YYYY] 📅

Email address* [ ]

Country where head office is located* [ ]

Total number of employees*   ○ 1-49   Include full time, part time, casual and contract employ
○ 50-199
○ 200 or more

Social networking sites used for marketing activities
☐ Facebook
☐ Twitter
☐ Pinterest
☐ LinkedIn
☐ Vine
☐ Instagram
☐ Tumblr
☐ Google+

Can we send you information about special offers and new products?*   ○ Yes   ○ No   You can opt-out at any time.

[Apply] [Cancel]   *Must be answered

4-65. Questions should be far enough apart that it's clear where one ends and the next one starts

Remember how the focus of a user's vision is about nine characters wide? Well, this means question-level help that's on the right side of a field often won't be seen:

4-66. Their focus on fields means many users won't even see the question-level help in this form

We could move the question-level help underneath the field, but that means users might not see it until after they've answered. It's also less accessible.

4-67. Question-level help below the field is not especially usable or accessible

Formatting instructions—like the DD MM YYYY on date of birth—should go above the field:

BUSINESS BANK ACCOUNT APPLICATION

☺
Enders Bank

Business trading name* [   ]

ABN* [   ] You must have an Australian Business N

Given name* [   ]

Family name* [   ]

Date of birth* DD MM YYYY
[ ] [ ] [   ] 📅

Email address* [   ]

Country where head office is located* [   ]

Total number of employees*   O 1-49   Include full time, part time, casual and contract employ

O 50-199

O 200 or more

Social networking sites used for marketing activities   ☐ Facebook

☐ Twitter

☐ Pinterest

☐ LinkedIn

☐ Vine

☐ Instagram

☐ Tumblr

☐ Google+

Can we send you information about special offers and new products?*   O Yes O No   You can opt-out at any time.

[Apply] [Cancel]   * Must be answered

4-68. Formatting instructions positioned above the field

Other question-level help should go below the label. See the ABN, employee and marketing questions for examples of this:

BUSINESS BANK ACCOUNT APPLICATION

Business trading name*

ABN*
You must have an Australian Business Number
(ABN) to apply for an Enders bank account.

Given name*

Family name*

Date of birth*   DD   MM   YYYY

Email address*

Country where head office is located*

Total number of employees*   O 1-49
Include full time, part time, casual and   O 50-199
contract employees.
O 200 or more

Social networking sites used for marketing   ☐ Facebook
activities   ☐ Twitter
☐ Pinterest
☐ LinkedIn
☐ Vine
☐ Instagram
☐ Tumblr
☐ Google+

Can we send you information about special   O Yes   O No
offers and new products?*
You can opt-out at any time.

Apply   Cancel   *Must be answered

Enders Bank – Business Bank Account Application
Enders Bank

4-69. Other question-level help positioned below the label

Always Show Question-level Help

Many people feel the need to hide the help on their forms, despite this being decidedly unhelpful.

For instance, it's fairly common to see question-level help hidden behind an icon:

* When was your passport issued?

| Select day ▼ | Select mo ▼ | Select yea ▼ |

* When does your passport expire?

| Select day ▼ | Select mo ▼ | Select yea ▼ |

* What is your passport number?

* What country are you a citizen of?

| Select country ▼ |

4-70. On this form, question-level help is hidden behind a question mark icon

Some forms show question-level help only when the user puts focus into the relevant field:

What level of investment are you seeking?

The level of investment you seek needs to be backed up by your financial projections in your pitch deck. Be sure to provide details about equity being offered for the investment.

Note: we do not have any grants available.

Do you have a Minimum Viable Product? *   ☐ Yes   ☐ No

Do you have a Viable Product? *   ☐ Yes   ☐ No

Do you generate revenue? *   ☐ Yes   ☐ No

4-71. The question-level help (speech bubble at right) only appears when the user hovers over (on desktop) or taps (on mobile) the dropdown box

Don't be tempted to follow these trends. They have problems such as:

Because the help is hidden, the user has to make an extra effort to seeit.

- Because it requires extra effort, and users have learned (unfortunately) that much "help" on the web isn't particularly helpful, there's a good chance the help *won't* be seen, in turn increasing errors and reducing data quality.
- Hidden help may not work on touch devices (e.g. if the help shows only on hover, which doesn't exist on touch devices).
- Because space is still needed to show the help, there are no real "savings" from hiding the help behind an icon. (The alternative of a modal window, or pop-up, to display the help is best avoided, too, as discussed in "Modal Windows" in Chapter 5.)
- You don't know when the user needs the help, and it may be too late once they have put focus in the field.

Instead, always show the question-level help right there on the form. If it's particularly long, you can convey the main points within the form and then include a link to more detail.

Finally, when we use checkboxes and radio buttons, we need to make sure the labels are close to the right button or box. If they're too far away, things get confusing, particularly if you aren't shading the touch area:

**Can we send you information about special   O Yes O No
offers and new products?***
You can opt-out at any time.

4-72. The distance between the labels "Yes" and "No" and their respective radio buttons means the user has to stop and think

Here's an even more extreme illustration of poorly spaced labels on radio buttons:

How likely is it that you would recommend Wufoo to a friend or colleague? *
⦿ 0 – Not at all ◯ 1 ◯ 2 ◯ 3 ◯ 4 ◯ 5 ◯ 6 ◯ 7 ◯ 8 ◯ 9 ◯ 10 – Extremely

4-73. It's likely that many users will give an unintended rating, given the poor spacing here

Text Box Widths

While we're adjusting spacing, let's fix up our text box widths.

At the moment, aside from the text boxes for date of birth, all our text boxes are the same width:

BUSINESS BANK ACCOUNT APPLICATION

4-74. Text boxes all the same width

However, the width of a text box tells the user what sort of information is needed. The user experience will be better if we make the sizes proportional to the expected information (as we have, in fact, already done with date of birth):

4-75. Text boxes adjusted to have width proportional to typical answers

Note we're talking about *visual* width here, not acceptable number of characters. The email address field may have a visual width as shown, but should still accept up to 256 characters.

Empty Text Boxes

Another important aspect of text box spacing is the space they have *inside*. This empty space is how users know they need to type something in there.

Way too many forms have text boxes that *aren't* empty. The two main culprits are:

1. background color
2. placeholder text.

No Background Color

Do not give your fields a background color. Background color in fields makes them look like buttons (just as buttons without background color look like fields):

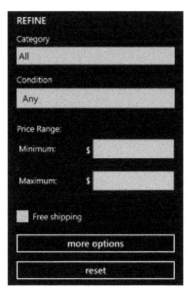

4-76. On this form, background color makes fields look like buttons, and vice versa

A simple border on four sides is enough to show users where to type:

Email address

We'll send your order confirmation here

First name

Last name

Password

Must be 6 or more characters and contain at least 1 number

4-77. You don't need much to show users where their answers go

Just make sure your border can be seen:

TITLE *

SELECT

FIRST NAME *   LAST NAME *

ADDRESS *

STATE *   SUBURB *   POSTCODE *

SELECT

EMAIL *

?

e.g. XXXXXXXXXX@davidjones.com.au

TELEPHONE *

?

e.g. 04XX XXX XXX or 9XXX XXXX

4-78. The field borders on this form are so light they're nearly impossible to see

No Placeholder Text

Even worse than a background color is putting text inside the field. **The only text that should appear inside a field is the user's answer!**

Such text, also known as **placeholder text**, is unfortunately far too common. Sometimes it's the field label:

first name

last name

email (this will be your username)

enter your password

confirm your password

4-79. This form's labels appear inside fields

Sometimes it's question-level help:

Birth Date

dd mmm yyyy

4-80. Question-level help shown inside fields

Sometimes it's just downright useless:

First name *

> First name

Email *

> Email address

Retype Email *

> Retype Email

Password *

> Your password

6-12 characters long

Retype password *

> Your password again

4-81. Pointless information inside fields

It's so important not to do this, I'm going to say it again. **Never include text inside your fields**. It dramatically worsens the form filling experience, as many users will:

- think the question has already been answered, triggering errors
- leave the placeholder text there, messing up your data
- not see the placeholder text before it disappears (especially if they watch the keyboard when typing)
- not be able to see all of the placeholder text, because it's limited by the visible width of the field
- forget what the label said
- forget what the question-level help said
- find the text too small to read
- be unable to review their answers

have greater trouble correcting errors.

Furthermore, text inside fields is often not accessible[13], and the placeholder attribute is not accurately supported in all browsers[14]. (It was once the case that placeholder text was *needed* for accessibility, because screen readers didn't always announce the form field. Now screen readers consistently use the `label` element to indicate the purpose of a field.)

"But it saves space!" some designers will protest. That's true. But that space is saved **at the expense of being able to actually fill out the form**. Don't do it. Just put your text outside your fields.

[13.] http://output.jsbin.com/vonesu/10/
[14.] http://caniuse.com/#feat=input-placeholder

 Float Labels

Alas, an approach called **float labels** has recently become popular, even appearing in Google's Material Design standard. With float labels, the label is initially shown inside the field:

| *First name** | *Last name** |

4-82. At the start, float labels look like any other placeholder text

When the field receives focus, the float label reduces in size, and moves further into or outside the corner:

| ┌ *First name** ────────── | *Last name** |

4-83. Putting focus inside the First name field floats the label up to the top left corner

Float labels are an admirable attempt to solve the problem of limited space on small screens. After all, the label is always visible:

| ┌ *First name** ────── | ┌ *Last name** ────── |
| Jessica   ✓ | |

4-84. Floated labels are still visible while the user fills out the form

But this approach still has too many issues for you to adopt it:

- fields still look filled initially, which means users will miss answering them, triggering errors
- the floated label is too small to read
- space isn't actually saved, because the field has to be made taller to fit the floated label
- animation is required, which increases page size and load time, and may not always work
- other types of fields—like checkboxes or radio buttons—can't use it
- long labels don't work with it
- users can struggle to understand which question they're up to, following distraction.

Until these issues are resolved, you should avoid using the float labels pattern. Instead, just place the label beside or above the field, and leave it there. (Emails accusing me of heresy can be sent to floatlabelsrock@formulate.com.au.)

Touch Tips

Remember our criteria for <u>"One Design to Rule Them All"</u> in Chapter 1?

Touch is an important consideration, so you should ensure your spacing meets the following rules of thumb:

- text boxes and buttons should be at least 2.75 rems high (a rem is a "root em"—see "Font sizing with rem" by Jonathan Snook[15])
- the touch area surrounding each vertical radio button or checkbox should also be at least 2.75 rems high.

Color

Currently, our form doesn't have much color at all:

[15.] https://snook.ca/archives/html_and_css/font-size-with-rem

4-85. At this stage, the only color on the form is the logo and the red asterisks indicating questions that require an answer

In terms of this part of the design, we're on the right track. I'll explain why.

Often, using color in an attempt to make a form "fun" or "interesting" can actually make the user experience worse:

Category
* SELECT CATEGORY — Employment Enquiry

Your Contact Info
* FIRST NAME
* LAST NAME
* EMAIL
* ADDRESS
* SUBURB
* POSTCODE
HOME NUMBER
* MOBILE NUMBER
* PREFERRED STORE — Please select...

Your Feedback
* FEEDBACK

Validation Code
* ENTER CODE FROM ABOVE

SUBMIT »

4-86. This very colorful form is more scary and confusing than fun

Some colors can even hurt people:

REGISTRATION FEES					
On or Before 2/13/2009			After 2/13/2009		
Members	Non-Members	Additional Speakers	Members	Non-Members	
$525	$675	$325	○ $600	○ $725	

UNEMPLOYED/STUDENT FEES (with proof of status)				
Members	Non-Members	Members	Non-Members	
$335	$385	○ $380	○ $440	

ASIS&T Member #: [_____]   Not a member? Join ASIS&T here!
And type "Applied For" in the box.
New ASIS&T Members, please register at the member rate.

Members of IAI,UPA, or AIGA, please enter the acronym and your member #
(e.g., "UPA 123456") and register at the ASIS&T Member rate.

PRE-CONFERENCE SEMINARS

SEMINARS (additional fee)	On or Before 2/13/2009	After 2/13/2009
WEDNESDAY, March 18		
1/2 Day AM Seminars		
Information Archeology (1/2 day, 8:30-12:30) Lorelei Brown, Hallie Wilfert	$300	○ $375
Career Workshop for Information Architects and Other User Experience Professionals (1/2 day, 8:30-12:30) Mario Bourque, Russ Unger	$300	○ $375
1/2 Day PM Seminars		
Information Architecture 3.0 (1/2 day, 2:00 - 6:00) Peter Morville	$300	○ $375

4-87. The fluorescent colors in this form may be hard for some people to look at

Be Very Careful with Color

Human beings are incredibly sensitive to color. Our brains process it without us even realizing, and we can't help noticing differences.

In our forms, we can use this feature of human biology to our advantage. **Reserve color for things that need it**, so they stand out in some way.

Here are some parts of a form that may benefit from color:

Buttons:

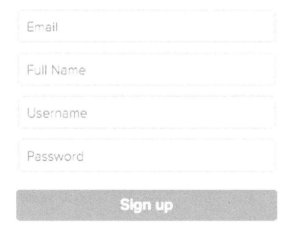

4-88. The only color on this form is the background of the button

Key messages, like errors:

Jessica@formulate.com.au

Password   Show

Please enter your password.

First name   Last name

4-89. Error highlighted in red

Links:

Username

[   ]

☐ I want to receive Etsy Finds, an email newsletter of fresh trends and editors' picks.

Register

By clicking Register, you agree to Etsy's Terms of Use and Privacy Policy. Etsy may send you communications; you may change your preferences in your account settings.

4-90. The links "Terms of Use" and "Privacy Policy" are blue

Progress indicators:

Type of application   Your details   **Contact details**   Organisation details   Review   Consent and declaration

4-91. Color helps differentiate past, current and future steps

Headings:

Personal Loan Application

It's easy to apply for a GE Money Personal Loan.

Your application should take **less than 15 minutes** to complete. If you'd prefer to speak to someone face to face, you can visit your local GE Money Branch.

Questions marked with an * are essential.

Step 1 of 4: Loan Details

Loan Details

How much would you like to * borrow?	$ [ ].00	Loans are available from $4,000.
What's the most you'd like to repay?	$ [ ] [per month ▼]	This will assist us in tailoring a loan to suit your needs.
What's the primary purpose of * the loan?	[Select ▼]	
Are you planning to use the loan for a secondary purpose?	[Select ▼]	
How many people are * applying?	⦿ One ◯ Two	

4-92. Color used to make headings stand out

Form backgrounds:

*Guest First Name	
*Guest Last Name	
*Email Address	
*Phone Number	
*Address	
*City	
State	
*Country	- Please Select -
*Postcode	

4-93. This form has a light blue background

Branding, like logos and standard headers, may also use color:

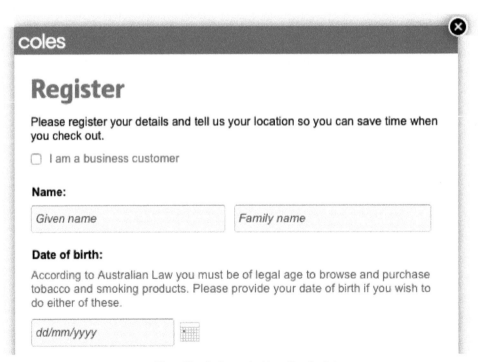

4-94. The red header is standard branding for Coles

You may have noticed that I didn't include the red asterisk of required field indicators (*) in the list of things that may use color. This is because I don't recommend the use of red asterisks to indicate required fields. See "Required Versus Optional Fields" below for more information.

Notice also how each of the examples above uses very little color overall. **The more color you use, the less it succeeds in making things stand out**:

4-95. This form uses color on almost every element, meaning none of them stand out

What Colors Should You Use?

Usually, your organization will have a palette of colors that you can refer to. Like my form design business, Enders Bank has a teal green as its main color, as you can see in the logo in the image below. Let's use that color to make the primary action button on our form distinctive:

BUSINESS BANK ACCOUNT APPLICATION

☺
Enders Bank

Business trading name* [_____]

ABN* [_____]

You must have an Australian Business Number
(ABN) to apply for an Enders bank account.

Given name* [_____]

Family name* [_____]

Date of birth*   DD   MM   YYYY
[__] [__] [____] 📅

Email address* [_____]

Country where head office is located* [_____]

Total number of employees*   ○ 1-49

Include full time, part time, casual and   ○ 50-199
contract employees.

○ 200 or more

Social networking sites used for marketing   ☐ Facebook
activities

☐ Twitter

☐ Pinterest

☐ LinkedIn

☐ Vine

☐ Instagram

☐ Tumblr

☐ Google+

Can we send you information about special   ○ Yes   ○ No
offers and new products?*
You can opt-out at any time.

[Apply] [Cancel]   *Must be answered

4-96. Our form now has all the color it needs

 Message Colors

You may want to reserve a version of each of the following colors for messages:

- red for errors
- orange for warnings
- green for success
- blue for information.

Color Blindness

Estimates vary, but it's likely that 4–10% of your web form's users will have some deficiency in their ability to perceive color (typically—but inaccurately—called **color blindness**). The most common form of color blindness is red–green, where distinguishing between these two colors is difficult.

Given this, you should **never want to rely solely on color to communicate something in your web form**. The form in figure 4-97 below uses red text for the labels of required fields, and black text for the labels of optional fields. Shame if you can't tell the red from the black! Not to mention how it makes the form look full of errors if you *can* see color well.

STUDENT 1 DETAILS

Student Number (If known)?

First name

Last name

Postcode

Address Line 1

Address Line 2

Home Phone

Work Phone

Mobile Phone

Email

Date of Birth (dd/mm/yy)

4-97. Color is the only way that required fields are indicated on this form, making it inaccessible to many users

A much better approach would be simply to tell people which fields are optional (as discussed in "Required Versus Optional Fields" below):

Company: (optional)

Title: (none)

First Name: Last Name:

4-98. Optional fields are marked as such

Similarly, error messages should be accompanied by a symbol or have background shading, instead of just red text (see also "Validation" in Chapter 5):

 To continue, please...

Answer these questions:

- "Does the car have any non-standard accessories or modifications?"

4-99. The exclamation mark symbol means users can visually tell this is an error message, even if they have a problem seeing colors

If you'd like to know more about color blindness, there are some great web resources out there, including simulations:

- We Are Colorblind[16]
- "Colour Accessibility" by Geri Coady[17]

Color Contrast

There's something even worse than relying on color to communicate to the user: insufficient color contrast. Not having enough contrast in your colors means even those of us with great vision can't *see* the different elements of the form:

[16.] http://wearecolorblind.com/
[17.] https://24ways.org/2012/colour-accessibility/

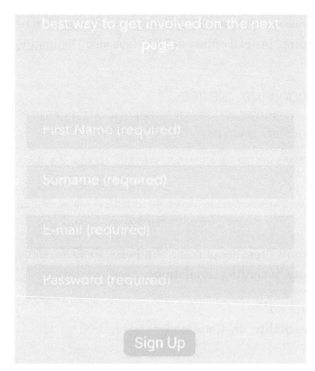

4-100. The green in the background of the form is too similar to the green in the background of fields, and both greens are too similar to the white used for text

This is an example of going way too far down the aesthetic end of the spectrum, at significant cost to the user experience. And it's popping up far too often these days:

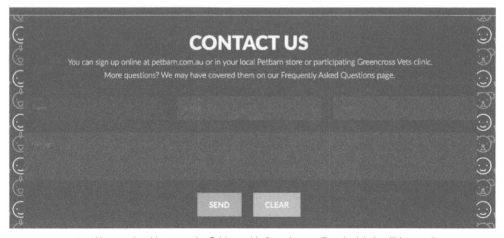

4-101. You may be able to see the fields on this form, but reading the labels will be tough

A particularly common contrast fail is the use of light grey on white backgrounds. Because it makes sites look clean and minimal, this color combination is quite popular at the moment. Pity it's completely unusable:

| First name |
| Last name |
| Email Address |
Will not be shared without your permission

| Password |
Must be at least 6 characters

| Password confirm |
Re-type your password

4-102. The low contrast between grey and white makes this form hard to see

Your form elements must have sufficient color contrast. For some really practical tips on ensuring this, I recommend:

- "Integrating Contrast Checks into your Web Workflow" by Geri Coady[18]
- "Three common pitfalls for developers: colour contrast" by Julie Grundy[19]

In the meantime, stick with dark grey or black on a white background:

---

18. https://24ways.org/2014/integrating-contrast-checks-in-your-web-workflow/
19. http://simplyaccessible.com/article/pitfalls-colour-contrast/

4-103. The colors in our example form have sufficient contrast

Required Versus Optional Fields

The issue of marking required fields came up a few times while we were discussing color, so let's sort it out now.

Required fields are questions that the user must answer. Conversely, **optional fields** are questions that the user can choose not to answer.

There are many ways to tell users which fields are required and which are optional. I've seen everything from orange lozenges to grey stars, and even underlining!

4-104. Possibly the most bizarre way to indicate required fields on the web

The approach that seems most typical is a red asterisk:

4-105. Questions that must be answered have a red asterisk at the end of the label

However, there are problems with this approach:

- An asterisk is a symbol, which means there is a layer of abstraction between the thing and what it represents.
- As we know from exploring color, a red asterisk is very visually prominent—and disproportionately so, given it's relatively low priority.

- Many users don't even look to see whether the field is required, because the vast majority of form questions must be answered.
- If there's a large number of required fields, it can be hard to find the optional ones, because they're shown by the *absence* of something.
- The red asterisk is not always accessible.

On top of this, the instruction explaining the red asterisk is often written in jargon (e.g. "mandatory field", which is largely meaningless), and is often very unhelpfully placed at the end of the form.

A much better approach is to only indicate the optional fields:

1. Have an instruction, at the top of each screen, that says: "All questions must be answered, unless marked (optional)."
2. Add "(optional)" to the end of the label for every optional question.
3. Don't add any visual markers to required fields.

This approach is highly accessible and usable, while also reducing the amount of visual noise.

Here's our bank form busy with red asterisks:

BUSINESS BANK ACCOUNT APPLICATION

Enders Bank – Business Bank Account Application

Enders Bank

Business trading name*

ABN*

You must have an Australian Business Number (ABN) to apply for an Enders bank account.

Given name*

Family name*

Date of birth* DD MM YYYY

Email address*

Country where head office is located*

Total number of employees*
Include full time, part time, casual and contract employees.
O 1-49
O 50-199
O 200 or more

Social networking sites used for marketing activities
☐ Facebook
☐ Twitter
☐ Pinterest
☐ LinkedIn
☐ Vine
☐ Instagram
☐ Tumblr
☐ Google+

Can we send you information about special offers and new products?*
You can opt-out at any time.
O Yes   O No

Apply   Cancel

*Must be answered

4-106. Red asterisks to indicate required fields

Compare that with the simplified design with "(optional)":

4-107. Optional fields are indicated by "(optional)"

 Many Optional Questions

There are some legitimate situations where forms have far more optional questions than required ones. In this situation, simply reverse the advice:

1. Have an instruction, at the top of each screen, that says: "All questions are optional, unless marked (required)."
2. Add "(required)" to the end of the label for every required question.
3. Don't add any visual markers to optional fields.

Buttons

Buttons on forms are fairly straightforward. But it's worth mentioning that you probably want to a *hierarchy of actions* through your visual design. In other words, you want:

- your primary action to stand out the most
- your secondary action(s) to stand out less than the primary action
- your tertiary action(s) to stand out less than the secondary action(s).

In figure 4-108 below, this hierarchy has been achieved by:

- giving the primary action button a strong background color
- giving the secondary action buttons a subtle background color
- turning the tertiary action into a link, which is even less prominent than a button.

4-108. Styling conveys the different levels of the action hierarchy

Other ways to make the primary action button stand out include:

- using a large text size for the label
- using **bold** or ALL CAPS for the label
- using a stronger border or other more prominent styling
- making the button physically bigger

having more whitespace around it (which also helps those with motor impairments).

In our form, the primary action button already has a different background color. But let's increase the size of the button and the prominence of its label, just so it really stands out. We really don't want users to cancel, either, so let's make that a link:

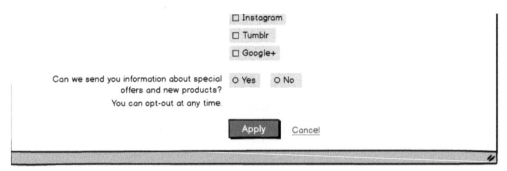

4-109. Creating an action hierarchy with our example form

 ## No Reset

An important tip regarding buttons: **don't include a reset button on your form!**

Such buttons are a hangover from the very early days of electronic forms. On most web forms, they do more harm than good. Too often, a form will be cleared instead of submitted.

There's no more surefire way to frustrate your users than setting them up to delete their own information!

Typography

We've almost finished laying out our form. All that's left is to tidy the typography.

Much of the typography of your form will be dictated by your organization. For example, your organization may have a style guide specifying that headings are to be set in the typeface Verdana, with all other text set in Arial.

If such guidelines exist, be sure to reference styles for the web, not print. And if there are no such guidelines, here are a few pointers.

Typeface

Body Text

To ensure that your form will work no matter what size the screen, choose a typeface that is easy to read at small and larger sizes. System typefaces like Georgia (serif) and Verdana (sans serif) fit this bill well.

Nowadays, you have access to a huge range of web fonts, but you should use them with care. Many are designed more for use on informational web pages, which comprise mostly headings and paragraphs of body text. This is different from a form, which has relatively few headings, hardly any paragraphs of body text, and a large number of question labels and question-level help.

We'll choose Helvetica Neue for our form:

4-110. Helvetica Neue typeface applied to our example form

In your web forms, it's best to:

- use the roman (that is, "base") font by default
- avoid italics or oblique (slanted) text, as it's hard to read on screen
- save bold for headings and emphasis
- avoid setting any text smaller than 10px, as many users will find it too hard to read.

Also, it helps the user if you distinguish question-level help from other parts of the question. A good way to do this is to make the question-level help slightly smaller or slightly lighter than the label and answer field text:

Username

You'll use this to log in to your account

Password

Choose a password   Confirm password

4-111. Question-level help text is lighter than label text

Let's apply this technique to our example form:

4-112. In our example form, question-level help text is lighter and smaller than label text

Headings

The styling of your headings should convey their position in the hierarchy. This means you want:

- your form title to be the most prominent heading
- your step headings to be less prominent than the form title
- your section headings to be less prominent than the step headings.

The simplest way to make text more prominent is by making it bigger, bolder or a different color:

Personal Loan Application

It's easy to apply for a GE Money Personal Loan.

Your application should take **less than 15 minutes** to complete. If you'd prefer to speak to someone face to face, you can visit your local GE Money Branch.

Questions marked with an * are essential.

Step 1 of 4: Loan Details

Loan Details

How much would you like to * borrow? $ [   ].00   Loans are available from $4,000.

What's the most you'd like to repay? $ [   ] per month ▼   This will assist us in tailoring a loan to suit your needs.

What's the primary purpose of * the loan?   Select ▼

Are you planning to use the loan for a secondary purpose?   Select ▼

How many people are * applying?   ● One ○ Two

4-113. The headings on this form are bigger, bolder and a different color from other text

However, when the user is on a smaller screen, we don't want our form title taking up half of it:

4-114. Heading sizes that work on larger screens may be impractical on smaller screens

Better to set up the form so it detects the smaller screen and makes the form title smaller:

4-115. The title of our form should be much smaller when viewed on mobile

This is another way we can apply responsive design to our forms, so they work no matter what the screen size.

Case

The term **case** refers to whether your text is written in:

- Sentence case (where just the first letter of the first word in each sentence is capitalized)
- Title Case (Where the First Letter of Most Words Is Capitalized)
- ALL UPPERCASE
- all lowercase.

Readers of English are most accustomed to sentence case, which is therefore likely to be read more quickly and accurately. So a good default is to use sentence case throughout your form, including headings.

Title case can be used for ... well ... titles (that is, headings). But title case is also harder to read than sentence case, so you should never use it in other parts of the form.

It's true that ALL UPPERCASE IS HARDER TO READ, but *not* because we lose the shapes of words. That's a rant for another time, but suffice it to say here that you should avoid uppercase at all costs. If nothing else, your users will appreciate you not shouting at them.

Except for the title, our example form is already in sentence case:

Enders Bank – Business Bank Account Application

BUSINESS BANK ACCOUNT APPLICATION

Enders Bank

Questions must be answered unless marked (optional)

Business trading name

ABN

You must have an Australian Business Number (ABN) to apply for an Enders bank account.

Given name

Family name

Date of birth   DD   MM   YYYY

Email address

Country where head office is located

Total number of employees
Include full time, part time, casual and contract employees.

○ 1-49
○ 50-199
○ 200 or more

Social networking sites used for marketing activities (optional)

☐ Facebook
☐ Twitter
☐ Pinterest
☐ LinkedIn
☐ Vine
☐ Instagram
☐ Tumblr
☐ Google+

Can we send you information about special offers and new products?
You can opt-out at any time.

○ Yes   ○ No

Apply   Cancel

4-116. Most of the text in our example form is in sentence case

The form title is a little shouty, so let's change that to title case:

Enders Bank – Business Bank Account Application

Business Bank Account Application

☺
Enders Bank

Questions must be answered unless marked (optional)

Business trading name

ABN

You must have an Australian Business Number (ABN) to apply for an Enders bank account.

Given name

Family name

Date of birth   DD   MM   YYYY   📅

Email address

Country where head office is located

Total number of employees   ○ 1-49

Include full time, part time, casual and contract employees.   ○ 50-199

○ 200 or more

Social networking sites used for marketing activities (optional)

☐ Facebook
☐ Twitter
☐ Pinterest
☐ LinkedIn
☐ Vine
☐ Instagram
☐ Tumblr
☐ Google+

Can we send you information about special offers and new products?   ○ Yes   ○ No

You can opt-out at any time.

Apply   Cancel

4-117. Title case used for the form title

All lowercase can work okay, as long as comprehension isn't compromised by the lack of capitalization. It's probably best only to use all lowercase if it's your organization's set style.

Line Length

There's just one last layout thing to do, and that's adjust the line length for text.

This is
an
example
of line
length
that
is too
short,
making
it hard
to get
a sense
of flow.

4-118. Short lines make it easy to lose your flow

It's easy for users to lose their place in long lines of text, but users also can lose their flow in very short lines of text, as you can see in the image above.

For general reading, the optimal line length is between 60 and 75 characters. It's a different type of reading, but still isn't a bad default for the field labels on our forms.

However, if your form's labels are mostly short, you may want to set line length to around 25–35 characters. This is the case with our example form:

Enders Bank – Business Bank Account Application

Business Bank Account Application

Enders Bank

Questions must be answered unless marked (optional)

Business trading name

ABN
You must have an Australian Business Number (ABN) to apply for an Enders bank account.

Given name

Family name

Date of birth   DD   MM   YYYY

Email address

Country where head office is located

Total number of employees
Include full time, part time, casual and contract employees.
- 1-49
- 50-199
- 200 or more

Social networking sites used for marketing activities (optional)
- Facebook
- Twitter
- Pinterest
- LinkedIn
- Vine
- Instagram
- Tumblr
- Google+

Can we send you information about special offers and new products?
You can opt-out at any time.
- Yes   - No

Apply   Cancel

4-119. Our example form has many shorter field labels, so lines are set to wrap if they're larger than about 35 characters

On mobile, however, you'll probably just want to set the lines to be 100% of the available width of the screen.

Contact Information

There's one last thing our form needs: contact information (in case the user needs help with the form).

You should include your organization's contact phone number on every screen of the form. That way, the user will be able to contact you, resolve an issue, and continue with the form without losing their progress.

Sometimes organizations are reluctant to do this, fearing a marked increase in workload for their support staff. Occasionally, great efforts are made to hide contact details from form users, in the belief this will keep calls under control.

It won't. If people need to contact you, they will. The only thing achieved by hiding contact information is ensuring users are even more annoyed by the time they get through. This in turn leads to more work for your support staff (as any experienced call center representative can tell you).

I haven't even mentioned how form submissions and overall satisfaction with your organization will decline, while error rates—which suck up even more resources from support staff—rise.

It's much better to nip any form issues in the bud before they can have such a negative impact on all parties. So include a contact phone number on every form screen:

4-120. A contact phone number is always visible, both reassuring the user and providing access to help if it's needed

What's Absent from Our Layout

We're about to review all that we've learned about what should be included in your form's layout. Before we do, let's quickly mention what should *not* be included:

- main site navigation, fat footers and other distracting, superfluous elements
- a jumbled, crowded or inconsistent mix of visual styles
- more branding than what's needed to give the user a sense of place.

By eliminating these elements, we've achieved a form that's simple, clean and attractive. And we know we can leave these elements out, because they don't aid the user in any way. As Luke Wroblewski says:

> any visual element that is not helping your layout ends up hurting it.

Review

Let's review the improvements we've made to the Enders Bank account application form.

This is how our form looked when we started learning about layout:

4-121. Our example form, before designing the layout, as seen on a larger screen

Things were even worse if we looked at it on a smaller screen, like a mobile:

4-122. Our example form, before designing the layout, as seen on mobile

Applying the principles for designing form layout, this is where we ended up on larger screens:

Enders Bank – Business Bank Account Application

Business Bank Account Application

Need help with this form?
Call 1300 130 130

☺ Enders Bank

Questions must be answered unless marked (optional)

Business trading name

ABN
You must have an Australian Business Number (ABN) to apply for an Enders bank account.

Given name

Family name

Date of birth   DD   MM   YYYY

Email address

Country where head office is located

Total number of employees
Include full time, part time, casual and contract employees.
○ 1-49
○ 50-199
○ 200 or more

Social networking sites used for marketing activities (optional)
☐ Facebook
☐ Twitter
☐ Pinterest
☐ LinkedIn
☐ Vine
☐ Instagram
☐ Tumblr
☐ Google+

Can we send you information about special offers and new products?
You can opt-out at any time.
○ Yes   ○ No

Apply   Cancel

4-123. Designed layout for our example form, as seen on a larger screen

And, thanks to responsive design, this is where we ended up on smaller screens:

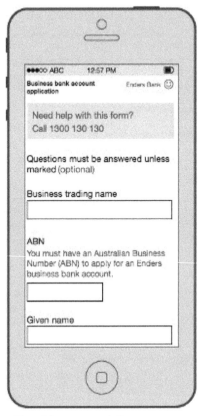

4-124. Designed layout for our example form, as seen on a smaller screen

A nice balance of aesthetics and user experience, don't you think?

Hopefully you also found it pretty straightforward getting there, following these steps:

- choose your answer field types
- line everything up to create a vertical path to completion, and connect labels to fields
- adjust the space between elements to help communicate their relationship
- resize text boxes to cue the required information
- make sure your text boxes are empty
- judiciously apply color, ensuring sufficient contrast
- mark the optional fields with a clear instruction, and remove any visual required indicators

- convey the hierarchy of actions through button and link design
- choose a good typeface for reading on screen, using different sizes and styles to convey the structure of the form
- put most text in sentence case
- set the line length to be not too small and not too large.

And we made sure that our form will work no matter the screen size—from desktop to mobile—by using responsive form design on the following:

- label placement
- text sizes
- button placement and sizing.

Our form is in great shape at this point, with well-designed questions and visuals. But we're not quite finished yet. The last piece of the form design puzzle is how things flow. From one question to the next, from filling in fields to fixing errors, the next chapter will cover the basics of form interactions.

Chapter **5**

Flow

Paper forms are static. Immobile, unresponsive, fixed. Forms come alive when they're on the web: questions can appear or hide, errors can be flagged and corrected, and the experience can be tailored to users and their needs.

In this chapter, we'll see how to best design all these user *interactions*, and more. Because we want the total user experience to feel smooth and painless—like gliding down a river—we'll call this aspect of form design **flow**.

Order

To begin, I want you to imagine you're at a party, which is being hosted by your friend Samira.

Samira introduces you to her friend Leo. Leo asks: "How do you know Samira?" You tell Leo you went to the same school, and share some of your adventures together. Before you know it, you're all laughing and swapping stories about Samira.

Samira then introduces you to another of her friends, Max. Max asks: "Do you believe in God?"

How do you react? Chances are, you're a bit thrown by Max's question.

The same sort of thing happens in forms. Have a look at the following image:

Q1. What is your firstname?

Q2. What is your surname?

Q3. What year were you born?

-- Please, select -- ▼

Q4. Are you:

◯ Female
◯ Male

next

5-1. This form starts with very personal questions

In both the form and the conversation with Max, the order is wrong. We expect to start with light, non-invasive questions. Very personal questions are usually reserved for later, when a relationship is established.

Having things in the wrong order completely throws the exchange and leads to discomfort. In both cases, you're likely to pause and hesitate, you may decide to give a vague answer or a non-answer, or you might even walk away. None of these things is good at a party, and they're downright failures when it comes to forms.

Putting things in the right order will do more than almost anything else to create an experience that flows. Unfortunately, the right order is often a matter of art as much as science. This is because **the right order depends so much on context, as well as user preference**. The best we can do is understand some foundational principles, and then try to implement them as much as possible.

Question Order

I used the analogy of a conversation deliberately. As we've indicated a few times already in this book, it helps to think of your form as a conversation. Imagine your form user is actually meeting face to face with someone from your organization. What order of questions makes sense in that exchange?

The form partly pictured in figure 5-1 above went on to ask for my feedback on the organization's activities (which centered around advocating for the environment). Perhaps, then, my feedback is the first topic they should have asked me about?

This brings us nicely to our principles for deciding question order.

Principles for Deciding Question Order

Follow How the User Thinks

The order of questions in your form should, as closely as possible, match the way things flow in the user's mind.

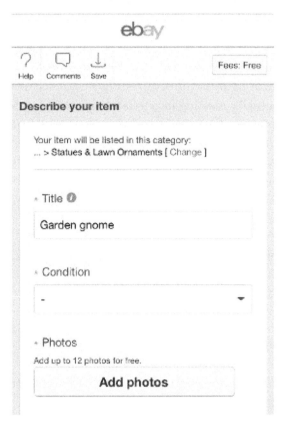

5-2. When selling an item online, the user expects to enter details about the item first, before details like price and postage. eBay has matched this order in their selling form.

Unless you're the one person on earth with genuine psychic powers, this means you need to do some careful research with your users.

Core Before Supplementary

Collect the information that's central to your form's purpose first, before collecting any supplementary information. That way, the most relevant and important data is provided when the user is freshest and most engaged with the form.

Where are you staying?

Location name

Address

123 Anywhere St., San Francisco, CA 94111 or
coordinates such as 47.616091, -122.197038

Need more help?

Description

How long are you staying?

Arrival date

22/6/2016

Arrival time

Timezone

Automatic Timezone

Departure date

dd/mm/yyyy

Departure time

Stay details

Number of guests

Number of rooms

Confirmation #

Room description

5-3. Adding accommodation to a journey, on travel-planning website TripIt. Core details like the name and location
are entered first, before supplementary information like number of rooms.

Easy Before Difficult

Ask simpler and less intrusive questions before complex and more intrusive
questions. This eases users into the process instead of bombarding them with
hard stuff up front. It also ensures users are more committed before being
presented with questions that may otherwise have tempted them to turn away.

1. Loan Details

2. Your Details

3. Employment Details

4. Financial Details

5-4. This progress indicator from a personal loan application shows that easier questions—like contact details—are asked before more challenging questions—like financial details.

Related Together

Remember our principle of <u>proximity</u> from Chapter 4? It stated that related elements should be near each other. The same principle applies to question order. The more related questions are, the closer they should be to each other in the form.

My contact details

My payment details

Email address

Card number

Confirm email address

CCV number ⓘ

Country

AUSTRALIA

Expiry date

MM ⏷   YYYY ⏷

Street Address

Please issue a receipt in...

◉ My name ○ My organisation's name

Please send my receipt via...

◉ Email ○ Post

Suburb (a selection will display as you type)

Phone number

○ Home ○ Work ○ Mobile

5-5. On this donation form, all questions about how to contact the user are near each other, and all payment-related questions are near each other

Be Consistent

Try not to change the order of questions from one part of the form to another.

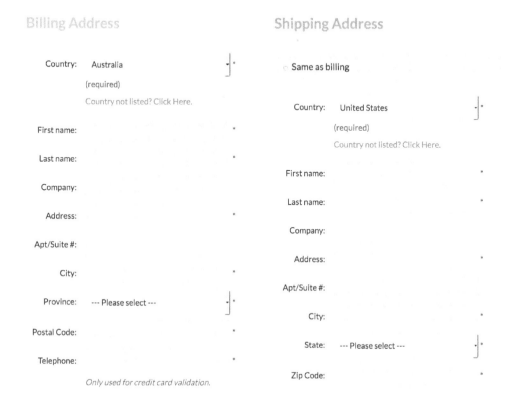

5-6. The order of address parts doesn't change between billing and shipping.

This applies to answer fields too. For instance, if you have a number of "yes"/"no" questions, try not to swap the order of the "yes" and "no" fields partway through.

Principles, Not Rules

You probably won't ever be able to apply all of these principles at the same time, in the same form. For this reason, there are principles, not hard-and-fast rules.

For instance, think about a bank loan application that collects the following information:

- specifics of the loan being requested (borrowing amount and repayment period)
- who is requesting the loan (identification)
- the applicant's income, expenditure, assets and liabilities (information for assessing the request)
- employment status and other demographic details (supplementary information for marketing and possibly also for assessing the request).

Should we put identification first—following the "easy before difficult" principle—or should it go near the end, to ensure we collect "core before supplementary"? Using the principle of "related together", do we put income and assets together, because they're about money coming in, or do we put income and expenditure together, because they're two sides of the same coin?

As you can see, a number of different—but all seemingly logical—orders can be used. But none implement all of the principles together.

This example also nicely demonstrates the value of user research. After all, what matters most is not what order works for *you*, but what works for your target audience. The only way to find this out is by conducting research with them.

 Tab Order

Some people will fill out your form using only the keyboard to navigate around it. This includes people who:

- don't have a mouse with them (e.g. are using a tablet device)
- just prefer not to use the mouse much (e.g. developers)
- are using assistive technology (e.g. people using a screen reader).

Make sure your form works for these people too, by setting the tab order to match the *visual* order in which questions, buttons and other elements are presented. There's nothing worse than clicking "Cancel" because the "Buy" button was skipped in the tab order!

Screens

Once you've ordered your questions, you'll want to decide how many screens to show them on.

Three Different Ways to Split over Screens

At one extreme, you can put all the questions on one (possibly long) screen. At the other extreme, you can show just one question per screen. In between is the option of having multiple screens, each with multiple questions.

These three health insurance quote forms illustrate the different approaches:

All questions on one screen:

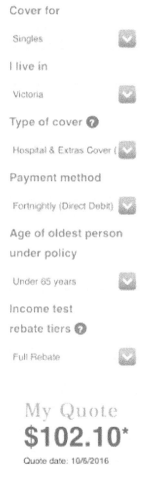

5-7. For this quick quote, only one question is shown on the screen at a time

Only one question per screen:

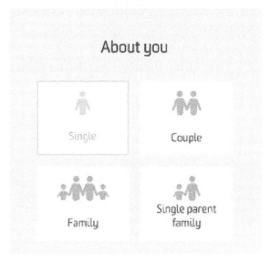

5-8. For this quick quote, all the questions are shown on the one screen

Multiple questions on multiple screens:

5-9. In between the other two extremes, we see here one screen from a quick quote that is broken up across several screens

Deciding the Number of Screens

Each approach has a number of advantages and disadvantages, which I won't go into here. Instead, I'll offer this simple formula:

1. Find out the most common screen sizes—including mobile and tablet—for your target audience (that is, the sizes that are used by at least 60% of people who'll use your form).
2. If the form can fit on three or fewer screenfuls of the most common sizes, leave it as one screen.
3. Otherwise, break the form up into separate screens, one step per screen (more on this below).
4. Avoid having more than seven screens.

This approach optimizes the user experience for the majority, while saving you from investigating how your form will look on the thousands of different resolutions, operating systems and devices on the market.

Multi-step (Screen) Forms

If you have multiple screens, you'll have one step of the form on each. How do you decide what constitutes a step? You should let the questions tell you.

Working with the questions in their proposed order, look for natural groupings and divisions. These give you a good starting place for steps.

For example, in our bank loan process, these might seem like sensible steps:

1. Identification
2. Income
3. Assets
4. Expenditure
5. Liabilities
6. Loan request
7. Supplementary information.

In this structure, the most related questions always appear in the same step. For example, name, address and phone number all appear in the Identification step.

But will users find it weird that some information about the person requesting the loan is collected in the first step, and the rest is collected in the last step? User testing is the only way to know.

It might actually be wise to test a slightly different set of steps:

1. Loan request
2. Income and assets
3. Expenditure and liabilities
4. Identification and supplementary information.

This second approach not only puts together all the information about the person requesting the loan, it has fewer steps so may seem less daunting to users. (Longer screens are the trade-off for fewer steps.) This order of steps also looks like a better fit with the principle of "core before supplementary". But again, only testing with users will confirm what works. It's also very likely that there's more than one suitable way.

 ## Keep it Together

The principle of natural groupings may lead to a change in the number of screens. For instance, even if the income section of our bank loan process contains more than three screenfuls of questions, we probably won't want to split the section up over two screens/steps.

Don't feel that you're stuck with the number of screens you landed on when looking at common screen sizes. This technique should flex to fit natural question groupings.

One Question per Screen

Recently, there's been a minor resurgence in designing forms to have only one question per screen. (I say "resurgence", because this is how wizards work, and wizards were very popular in the early days of personal computing.)

5-10. A form with one question per screen

One question per screen can help users focus on the task at hand, especially those with low digital literacy or people using a small screen. Conversely, they can make performance and completion times worse, especially on mobile, as more pages need to be loaded.

All in all, we're only at the beginning of understanding how this approach impacts on user experience, especially for longer forms.

If you have the resources, you may wish to test your form designed with one question per screen. If you do, please share the results with the community! Otherwise, designing your form to have multiple questions per screen is going to create a user experience that's at least no *worse* than those of the last few years. Plus, the lion's share of web forms currently do have multiple questions per screen, so this approach will be familiar. Familiarity goes a long way toward a positive user experience.

Progress Indicators

Until now, it was a given that a form with multiple steps should have a progress indicator, like the one shown below:

5-11. Progress indicator from a car insurance form

After all, wouldn't users want to know where they're at, what's to come, and what's behind them?

Some recent research[1] suggests that progress indicators may not be as necessary as we think, and may even detract from the user experience. This research is very new, and more is needed before we throw out our progress indicators. But if you have the resources, you may like to test your form without a progress indicator, and see what happens. (If you do, be sure to measure both objective and subjective indicators of user experience, like completion time and satisfaction respectively.)

If you include a progress indicator, at a minimum it should:

- indicate which step the user is currently on
- indicate the total number of steps.

So your progress indicator may be as simple as this:

5-12. Progress indicator giving a sense of current and overall position

This is a particularly good approach for mobile forms, as it doesn't take up much space.

If you want to flesh out your progress indicator—perhaps only on large screens—then visually distinguish between three different steps:

- steps the user has completed

---

[1] https://designnotes.blog.gov.uk/2014/07/07/do-less-problems-as-shared-spaces/

◌ step the user is on

◌ steps ahead of the user.

Here's an example:

5-13. This progress indicator has steps in three different states: past, current ("Delivery") and future.

If you show the name of each step in the progress indicator, make sure the wording exactly matches the heading shown on the respective screens:

5-14. Step headings and labels in the progress indicator should match

You may be tempted to indicate progress using percentages, like this:

5-15. Percentage progress indicator

Alas, **on forms, percentage-based progress indicators are a terrible idea**. They seem to offer greater precision and thus be more informative. Yet the reality is they have *less* information. And for the form user, this vagueness is a problem.

Is the percentage a calculation of time, steps, questions, or effort? What if one step has a particularly large number questions compared to the others, or a new step appears because of answers given in earlier steps? Even if the interface gives the user clarity around these points, you'll find it difficult to resolve them yourself. Instead, stick with step-based, labeled, progress indicators, combined with up-front eligibility questions (see the "Eligibility" section below).

Finally, your progress indicator must be *honest and transparent*. For instance, don't pretend there are 3 steps when there are actually 5. Figures 5-16 through 5-18 below show three distinct screens presented to the user, all under the heading of a single "Log In" step:

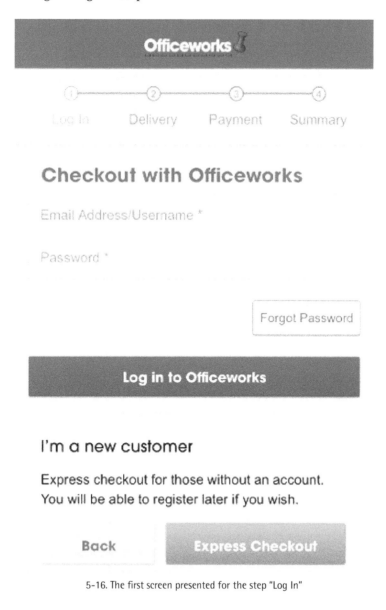

5-16. The first screen presented for the step "Log In"

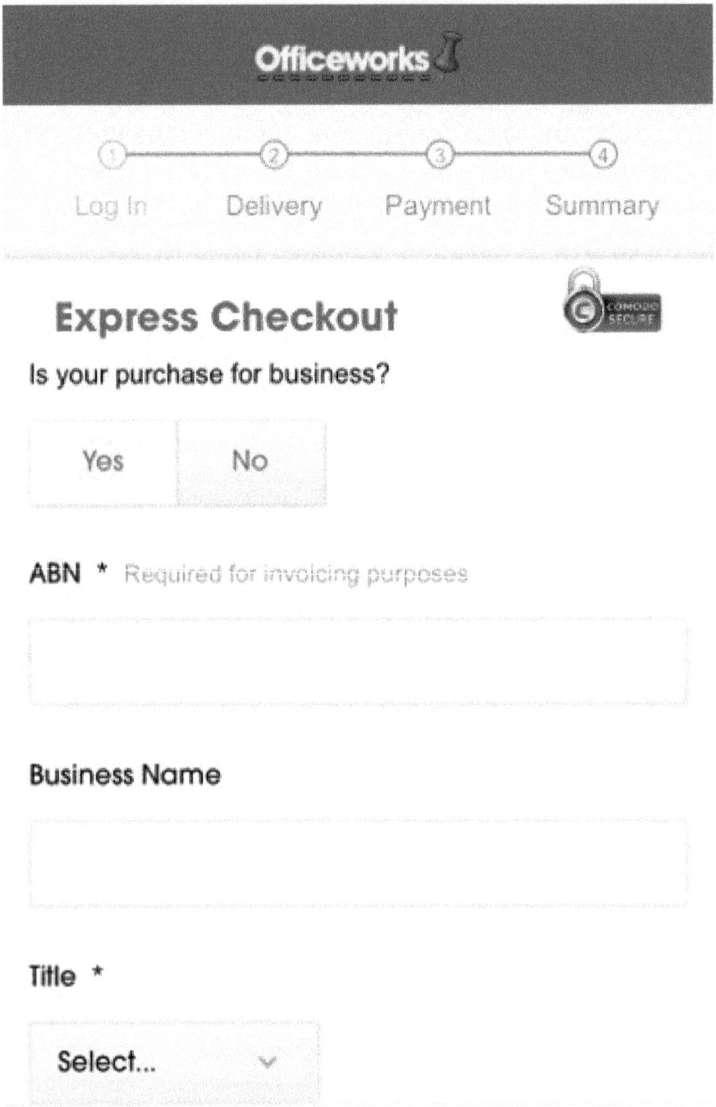

Officeworks
1
2
3
4
Log In
Delivery
Payment
Summary
Express Checkout
COMODO SECURE
Is your purchase for business?
Yes
No
ABN * Required for invoicing purposes
Business Name
Title *
Select...

5-17. The second screen presented for the step "Log In"

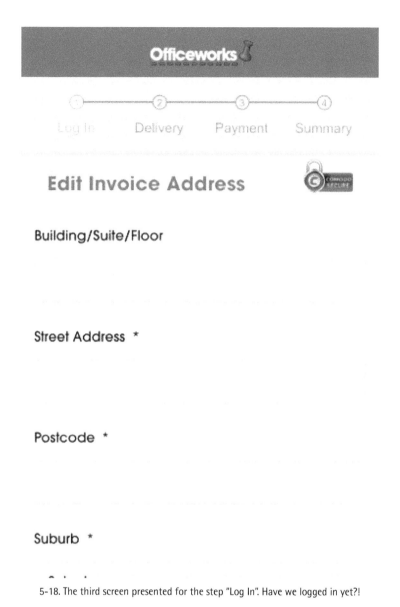

5-18. The third screen presented for the step "Log In". Have we logged in yet?!

Misleading or deceptive progress indicators may be a tempting way to draw more users into your form, but they'll only lead to greater abandonment, dissatisfaction and distrust.

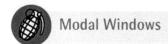

Modal Windows

Modal windows are windows that pop up on top of other windows:

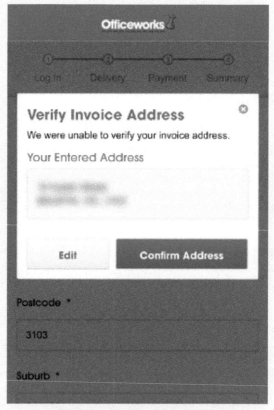

5-19. A modal window on a mobile form

In your forms, it's best to keep modal windows to a minimum, because they:

- can make it hard for users to know where they are and what's going on, especially those with cognitive disabilities
- often don't work well on mobile
- may disappear off screen, particularly if the screen is small
- may not be seen by people using screen magnifiers
- may not be announced by screen readers.

Before and After

At this point, we've settled the structure of the form, by deciding on:

- the order of questions
- the number of screens
- the content of each screen
- what progress indicator to use, if any.

Our form is really coming together. Nevertheless, what happens *just* before your form starts, and *just* after it finishes, is as important as the form itself.

We manage the "just before" via a **gateway screen**, and the "just after" via a **confirmation screen**. Let's have a look at these.

Gateway Screen

Many web forms don't actually need a gateway screen, because they're so small and typical. This includes:

- search
- sign up or log in
- contact us
- simple ecommerce checkouts.

Get started with a free account

Create a free MailChimp account to send beautiful emails to customers, contributors, and fans. Already have a MailChimp account? Log in here

Email

> freddie@mailchimp.com

Username

Password   👁 Show

- One lowercase character
- One uppercase character
- One number
- One special character
- 8 characters minimum

By clicking this button, you agree to MailChimp's Anti-spam Policy & Terms of Use.

5-20. This is such a short and familiar form, it doesn't need a separate gateway screen

On such forms, a gateway screen would be overkill. For most other forms, however, **the only entry point should be a single gateway screen on your website**.

The gateway screen should *briefly*:

- explain what and who the form is for
- warn users of any external sources of information they'll need (e.g. their passport or driver license)

warn users of any equipment they'll need (e.g. a printer or a credit card)

share the average time to complete the form (if known), so the user can make an informed decision about when to fill it out

let users know whether they'll be able to save when part way through and resume later, if the form will take more than 5–10 minutes

provide a *summary* of any legal considerations, including privacy, terms and conditions, with links to more detailed information.

The gateway screen should also:

include a prominent call-to-action button (e.g. "Start now" or "Begin application")

be indexed and appear in search results (the form itself should not)

be part of the website's navigation

be the page that all references to the form point to, regardless of whether those references are internal or external to the website

not be included in the progress indicator (because it's before, not part of, the form).

In my experience, gateway screens rarely meet all these criteria. They often do some things well (like a prominent call to action) but are missing other important components (such as a warning to users about external sources of information).

Here are some examples of gateway screens that have at least *some* of the necessary features:

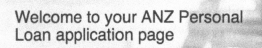

Welcome to your ANZ Personal Loan application page

 It takes about 10 minutes to complete

 Times out in 15 minutes if left unattended

 When you're finished we'll give you a response in 60 seconds

What you'll need

- Income, employment and financial commitment details
- Driver's license (if you have one)
- Your ANZ account number or Customer Registration Number (if you have one)

What happens after you apply?

- Confirmation will be sent to your nominated email address explaining next steps
- If your loan is approved, you will be sent a Letter of Offer
- Once you have accepted our offer, the funds will be available to you

Number of applicants

| One | Two |

Start

5-21. This gateway screen prepares the user well, but the call to action isn't positioned well

Tax your vehicle

Tax your car, motorcycle or other vehicle using your reminder letter (V11).

If you don't have a reminder letter, you can use:

- a V5C registration certificate (log book) that's in your name - get a replacement if you don't have one
- your new keeper supplement (V5C/2) if you've just bought the vehicle
- your 'last chance' warning letter

Other ways to apply

By phone

Telephone: 0300 123 4321
Find out more about call charges

At the Post Office

Go to your local Post Office ☑ that deals with vehicle tax. You'll need payment for your vehicle tax and one of the following:

- your vehicle tax reminder letter (V11)
- a V5C registration certificate (log book) in your name
- a new keeper supplement (V5C/2), if you've just bought the vehicle

You may also need:

- your MOT test certificate (must be valid when the tax starts)
- a valid reduced pollution certificate

In Northern Ireland ☑ you'll also need an insurance certificate or cover note.

5-22. Another example with nice brief introduction and a prominent call to action. This gateway screen also warns the user about external sources (reminder letter and its alternatives).

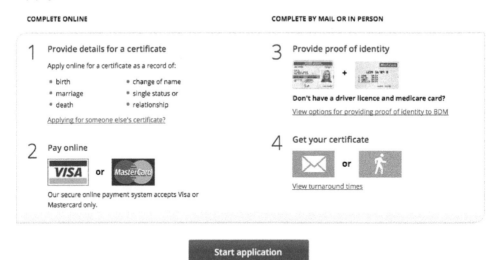

Home > Apply for a certificate

Apply for a certificate

COMPLETE ONLINE

1 Provide details for a certificate

Apply online for a certificate as a record of:

- birth
- change of name
- marriage
- single status or
- death
- relationship

Applying for someone else's certificate?

2 Pay online

VISA or MasterCard

Our secure online payment system accepts Visa or Mastercard only.

COMPLETE BY MAIL OR IN PERSON

3 Provide proof of identity

Don't have a driver licence and medicare card?

View options for providing proof of identity to BDM

4 Get your certificate

View turnaround times

Start application

In line with the *Privacy and Data Protection Act 2014*, the Registry is collecting information in this form to determine your eligibility to obtain the requested certificate and to prevent fraud. A copy of the Registry's Privacy Policy is available at bdm.vic.gov.au

If you do not provide all of the information requested, particularly that relating to the reason the document is required and your relationship to the registered person, then you may not be provided with a certified copy of the certificate.

5-23. This gateway screen lives on the main website, can be found via search, and sits in the navigation. There's a nice big call to action. The screen also explains what the form is for, warns that card payment and proof of identity are needed, and includes a legal summary.

Having said that, with more complex forms it often becomes necessary to ease the user into the process, rather than overload them with too much information up front. Remember how we talked about "Easy Before Difficult" above? The idea is to gradually draw the user into the form filling experience. The equivalent with gateway screens is to spread information over a few initial steps. If you think your form may fit into this category, it's crucial that you test with users to find out exactly when the different pieces of information are needed.

Let's talk about you!

Information Disclosure: To offer you an accurate quote, we will use information from you and other sources, such as your driving, claims and credit histories. Please review our Privacy Policy and information about our use of consumer reports. Auto insurance prices and products are different when purchased directly from Progressive or through agents/brokers.

Please answer our questions accurately, as accidents and violations discovered only by ordering consumer reports cause rates to be higher than if disclosed by you.

Okay, start my quote.

No, thanks.

5-24. This is an example of a gateway screen combined with the start of the form, so that information can be given progressively. It includes a prominent call to action, the legal summary, and an indication of the form's length (via the progress indicator at the top)—albeit without an indication of the time the process will take.

Confirmation Screen

The confirmation screen lets users know:

- that they have finished filling out the form (yay!)

that submission of their answers was successful (double yay!)

what their receipt or reference number is (if relevant)

whether confirmation or a copy of their filled out form has been emailed to them

what's going to happen next

how to track the processing of the form or get further information

what further actions, if any, the user has to take

where they might want to go next (so it's not a dead end).

This may seem like a lot of information, but it can be provided succinctly, as this example shows:

Thank you, Jessica

Your order is complete. We have emailed you an order summary and confirmation.

Your order number is 153132444

When will I receive my order?

Your order will be dispatched for Next available delivery day to the following address:

Ms. Jessica Enders

If you have any questions, please call customer service on **1300 OFFICE** or **1300 633 423** between 8am and 7pm EST, Monday to Friday.

5-25. A confirmation screen at the end of an ecommerce form

Here's another great confirmation screen, also from a mobile transaction:

Thank you for purchasing with SkyBus

Your ticket is valid for three months from the date of purchase. Tickets must be presented at the time of travel. You can print your ticket or present it on your smartphone.

Print your ticket

Your PDF ticket can be printed and includes a tax invoice.

Smartphone ticket

You can also present your ticket on your smartphone. Click the link below while on your smartphone to view your ticket/s onscreen.

A link to this page has been sent to the email address you provided.

Transaction summary

Invoice reference:
W6014768D1F068DC075DE8
Transaction date: 07 Dec 2015, 12.34 p.m.
Payment amount (AUD): $96.00
Receipt number: 01596795

5-26. A confirmation screen on mobile

The confirmation screen is also an opportunity to thank the user for their efforts and create a sense of reward. MailChimp is well known for having confirmation screens that do just that:

Rock on!

Your email has been scheduled.

Your campaign will be sent on 4/29/14 8:00AM.

Get The Mobile App To Track Reports

Make a paper buddy while you wait for your reports to come in.

5-27. This confirmation screen makes the user feel like a star

Finally, the confirmation screen is also a good place to collect feedback on the form-filling process. A simple yet effective way to do this is by asking the Single Ease Question (SEQ)[2]:

---

2. http://www.measuringu.com/blog/single-question.php

Overall, this task was?

Very						Very
Difficult						Easy
○	○	○	○	○	○	○

5-28. Single Ease Question, as developed by Jeff Sauro and Joe Dumas

Answering the SEQ should be optional. If you want to know a bit about what's behind the ratings that users give, add an (optional) comment field.

 Email Confirmation

If your form collects the user's email address, also send them a copy of the confirmation. This gives them something they can refer to permanently.

Eventbrite

Find events   My Tickets

Hi Jessica, this is your registration confirmation for
UX Australia 2016

Organised by UX Australia

Registration summary

                    or

Mobile Summary   Paper Summary

              Open the email attachment
or download here

Message from UX Australia

The event organiser has provided the following information:

Event Information

5-29. An email confirmation of successful event registration

Review Screens

If submitting your form will have a significant impact (such as deducting money from the user's bank account), or the form is multi-step, consider having a **review screen**.

Check your answers before sending your application

Organisations involved

Exporter	Exporter name First line of address Second line of address Contact: Contact Name Tel: 01234 567 890 Email: email@email.com	Change
Producer	Producer name	Change
Site of export	Site of export name	Change
Importer	Importer name First line of address Second line of address Contact: Contact Name Tel: 01234 567 890 Email: email@email.com	Change
Recovery facilities	Recovery facilities name	Change
Recovery site	Recovery site name	Change

Now send your application

By submitting this notification you are confirming that, to the best of your knowledge, the details you are providing are correct.

Accept and send application

5-30. Example of a review screen, from the UK Government Digital Service

The review screen is the last screen of the form, appearing just before the confirmation. As the name suggests, it provides users with a chance to review their answers, all in one place, before submission.

Review screens should present back the form questions, sections and steps, and the user's answers to them, in the same order as they appeared in the form. If you can, include a link to "Change" or "Edit", against each step, section or question, so the user can quickly jump to the relevant part of the form.

Validation

After order, the next most influential part of the interaction is error checking, also called **validation**.

Two Types of Errors

With web forms, validation helps ensure that when the data comes to us, it's of better quality than it would be from a paper form. There are two types of errors you can check for:

1. **Errors of omission**: questions for which an answer was required, but not provided
2. **Errors of commission**: answers that are not right in some way.

Errors of Omission

Errors of omission are pretty straightforward: run a check to confirm there's an answer for every question that's not optional. Users should then be told which questions must be answered, but haven't been.

Jessica@formulate.com.au

Password   Show

Please enter your password.

5-31. The password field hasn't been filled out, resulting in an error of omission

Disabling the Primary Action Button

Some designers like to disable (or remove!) the primary action button until all required questions have been answered. The theory is that this prevents users from submitting the form when we know it's not ready.

It's a nice theory, but bad practice. **A disabled primary action button doesn't tell the user what's wrong, or how to fix it.** The user ponders: "Is there a bug with the form, or have I done something wrong?" Additionally, if grey has been used to color secondary action buttons, it may not even be clear that the primary action button *is* disabled.

A much better approach is to **always enable the primary action button**. If the form is submitted without all required questions answered, just report this as part of error messaging (see "Messages" below).

Errors of Commission

Any answer that isn't valid is an error of commission. This would include things such as:

- a date of birth in the future
- a negative number of guests for a dinner reservation
- a phone number with a letter in it
- a postal code that doesn't match suburb or town
- a street that doesn't exist
- a membership number that's missing a digit
- a password that isn't right for the username.

Email

> jessica.formulate.com.au

An email address must contain a single @

5-32. The user has typed "." instead of an "@", resulting in an error of commission

Errors of commission are trickier than errors of omission. This is because:

- you have to make a choice about how much you check (that is, the breadth and depth of your validation rules)

you have to write precise rules for each error, some of which may be complex.

The choice about how much you check is about finding an optimal approach between two ends of a continuum:

- not validating enough, leading to the organization having to follow up with users after submission
- validating too much, which
    - takes a lot of design and coding resources
    - puts a significant burden on users, and
    - is likely to result in acceptable (but unanticipated) answers being flagged as errors.

Not validating enough is self-explanatory. A common example of validating *too* much is requiring users to enter data in just one format—the one that suits your database—rather than accommodating the various formats that make sense to them.

5-33. This field is highly inflexible

There's no reason for fields like credit card number and phone number to be inflexible like this. As we've said many times before, the form should work according to how the user thinks. Making it easy for answers to go straight into the database is not good validation. It's lazy coding.

 International Formats

Inflexible validation that doesn't cater for international formats is a very common form frustration. For instance, mobile (cell) phone numbers are formatted differently by different cultures, let alone by different individuals within the one culture. A study I conducted into how users enter Australian mobile phone numbers[3] found more than 40 variations, and the design of the study meant that this was probably just the tip of the iceberg in terms of *preferred* approaches.

We've also seen how dates in the United States are written differently from those in the United Kingdom and Australia. (Refer back to my "International Date Picking" warning in Chapter 4.)

As you write your validation rules, be aware of these differences, and ensure sufficient flexibility for your target audience. And remember, even if your form is about something specific to your country, people from overseas may still use it (e.g. booking local travel before arriving).

Back to our validation continuum. You'll find the sweet spot is checking for some very obvious or disastrous errors of commission—like an email address without an "@"—but not a lot more than that.

Inline Validation

Forms should always be checked for errors every time a screen of questions is submitted (which is called **server-side validation** in technical speak; see also the Warning below). In the last few years, however, some forms have included **inline validation**: answers are checked as soon as they're provided (a particular kind of **client-side validation**, in which validation tasks are handled by the browser).

[3.] http://www.formulate.com.au/blog/mobile-phone-numbers-in-electronic-forms

formulateid

••••

verify password

email

☐ remember me

☐ get the best of reddit emailed to you
once a week. learn more

SIGN UP

5-34. The user is halfway through this form, which has inline validation. The first answer has passed validation, but the second has failed.

Inline validation gives immediate feedback when there's an issue, and often also when there's not. For very short forms with few questions—such as the sign-up form in the image above—this is a good thing.

However, there are many implementation issues involved with inline validation, the most common being that the validation is performed too soon.

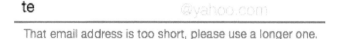

That email address is too short, please use a longer one.

5-35. This user was still typing the email address when the inline validation error message came up

If you look closely at most web forms using inline validation, you'll see they have this problem. Even Facebook wasn't immune: the company removed inline validation from its sign-up form after initially including it.

Another major problem is that it quickly gets very difficult to perform all validation inline. For instance, some answers may need to be checked against a large database stored on the server.

If you can't validate all answers inline, you'll have to include both inline and server-side validation in the one form. But this in turn leads to a most unpleasant experience, where a user passes the inline validation, and thinks all error checking has been done, only to receive yet more errors on submission. This might happen, for example, on a login form, where the username is judged by inline validation to contain acceptable characters, but then fails server-side validation because there's no matching account.

A third issue is that many users are watching their keyboard when they type, not their screen, so inline validation might not be seen.

As if all this weren't enough, inline validation on longer forms interrupts the form-filling process and makes for a much worse user experience. This is because, with inline validation, users have to repeatedly switch between two quite different mental modes: form filling and error correcting. This slows the user down, increases cognitive effort, and generally reduces user satisfaction.

Given all these issues, **I recommend *against* using inline validation**. It certainly should only be considered if:

- the form has a small number of questions (e.g. fewer than 10)
- the vast majority of validation rules can be checked inline.

For instance, you may want to use inline validation on a very short account registration form (see figure 5-36 below). In this situation, inline validation is a much faster way for users to go through the steps of:

- picking a username and checking to see if it's available
- choosing a password and checking to see if it meets the site's requirements.

Jessica Enders

info@formulate.com.au

••••|

Sign up

5-36. Inline validation can work well on very short registration forms

If you do use inline validation:

- all the rules about error messaging apply (discussed below in "Messages")
- you *must* give users time to enter their answers before the validation happens (unlike in figure 5-35 above)
- don't use the inline validation built into HTML5: it's a horrible user experience
- read more about it at "Inline validation in forms—designing the experience"[4] by Mihael Konjević.

 ## Never Rely Solely on Client-side Validation

As you likely already know, you should **never rely solely on client-side validation for anything important**—like something that might break your database if submitted in the wrong format, or that might open the site up to malicious attacks via injected code. Client-side validation is very easy to defeat if someone has nefarious aims. Server-side validation should always be present to prevent the entry of any problematic data or code.

Messages

Once we've done validation, we need to communicate errors to the user. Throughout the process, we also need to communicate other information, such as

---

[4.] https://medium.com/wdstack/inline-validation-in-forms-designing-the-experience-123fb34088ce#.vqbw1xole

warnings and success messages. The styling and interactivity of these messages can be just as important as the words used (see <u>Chapter 3</u>).

Error Messages

Recall the three components of an effective error message, described in <u>Chapter 3</u>:

1. convey that an error has occurred
2. be clear about exactly what and where the error is
3. tell the user what's required to correct or move past the error.

All of these components need to be worded in a polite and non-accusatory tone. But even if you've got your language right, your error messages may still trip up users if they aren't presented appropriately. Let's look at some examples.

Not putting the error message close to the corresponding field:

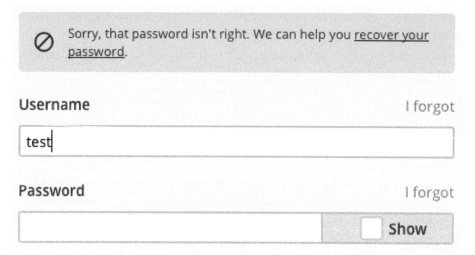

5-37. The error message here looks like it's about username, when it's actually about password. Nice wording though!

Making your error message too similar to the rest of the form:

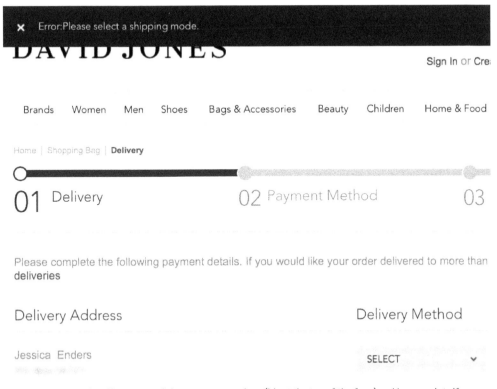

5-38. You get points if you spotted the error message here (it's at the top of the form) and bonus points if you noticed that it's actually wrong!

Not even *having* an error message:

5-39. The only thing on this form indicating that there's an error is the abstract red symbol to the right of the offending field

Using a popup/tooltip for the error message:

5-40. Popup/tooltip error messages are often not accessible or visible

Putting error messages off to the right where they may not be seen:

First Name [   ] ❌ Enter your firstname

Last Name [   ] ❌ Enter your lastname

Username [   ] ❌ Enter a username

Password [   ] ❌ Provide a password

5-41. The right-hand side of this form is outside the focus of our vision, so may not be seen

Using only color to show error fields:

Password

[   ]

Password strength:

5-42. If you have color-deficient vision—see Chapter 4—you may not be able to see that the field border is red. This approach also can't be used on fields other than text boxes.

It's actually very simple to present a great error message, as follows:

- use light red shading on the background of the whole question (which works for all answer field types)
- include an icon like an exclamation mark ("!")
- have the error message appear just before the corresponding question.

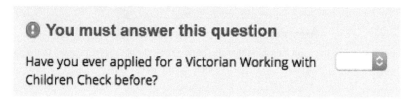

❗ You must answer this question

Have you ever applied for a Victorian Working with Children Check before?   [⬍]

5-43. An error message done well

Error messages should follow many of the general principles for layout that we discussed in Chapter 4—such as not having color as the only indicator of something.

For long forms on large screens, it's also important to summarize the errors at the top of the page, with an anchor link to each error within the form:

To continue, please...

Answer these questions:

- Is your postal address the same as your residential address?
- Residential address – Suburb or town

Provide a valid answer to these questions:

- Date of birth

5-44. A summary of error messages

If you don't include a summary, be sure to scroll the screen to the first error, so the user doesn't have to go hunting for it:

5-45. This form doesn't include a summary of error messages, but does scroll to the first error message on the screen

Errors Take Time

For designers and developers, validation and error messaging is often an afterthought. This is why so much of it is done poorly. A good rule of thumb is to take almost as much time to design a form's validation and error messaging as you spend on its layout.

Warnings

The difference between warnings and errors is that with a warning, users don't have to change their answers to proceed. In other words, warnings are less serious than errors.

The most common form warning you'll see is a message about session timeout:

Are you still there?

For your security, we will log you out in: **08:29**

I'm still working   I'm done, log me out

5-46. A visually well-designed timeout warning (although it could do with an icon as well)

(For more about designing timeouts, see the "Time Limits" section below.)

Another typical warning is when password strength is poor:

●●●●●●   ☐ Show

Weak ▬▬▬▬

5-47. A weak-password warning

Of course, if the form won't let the user proceed with a weak password, it becomes an error.

Warnings should follow the same design techniques as errors, but with less visual emphasis. Usually this means using orange in warnings in place of the red used in errors. Make sure there's enough difference between the two styles that users can easily tell them apart.

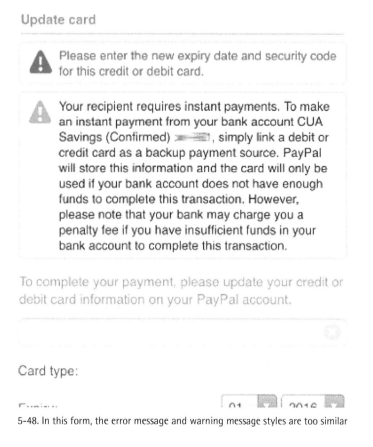

5-48. In this form, the error message and warning message styles are too similar

Success

The main success message on your form will be the one showing on submission. (Recommendations for this success message were given in "Confirmation Screen" earlier in this chapter.)

Your form may have other, lower-priority success messages. Examples include successful validation of an address, or confirming eligibility (discussed further in the "Eligibility" section below). These messages can be quite succinct—perhaps comprising just a suitable icon (such as a tick) and a single line of text (such as

"You're eligible for XYZ online"). Just make sure they're positioned appropriately (for example, next to the question that was validated, or at the top of the next step after eligibility).

System Processing

You may not have thought of it as a message, but those little dots circling around after submission are telling you the form is doing something:

Processing

We are now processing your order. Please be patient, this can take up to 3 minutes.

5-49. This excellent system-processing message uses animation together with informative text

Two key elements are needed to convey that the system is processing:

- a repeating animation
- preventing the user from interacting with the form.

In figure 5-49 above, the popup prevents the user from continuing to fill out the form. Sometimes the popup is supplemented by an overlay, so it's really clear the form can't be used:

Your Cover

Life Cover ⑦

< >

$50,000 $1,000,000

Total & Perm   PD)

Cover ⑦   ☐

Trauma Cover ⑦   ☐

Get a Quote

5-50. The animation on the center of this screen makes the form behind it fade, communicating that it can't be edited. Notice also how there's no text on this subtle system-processing message.

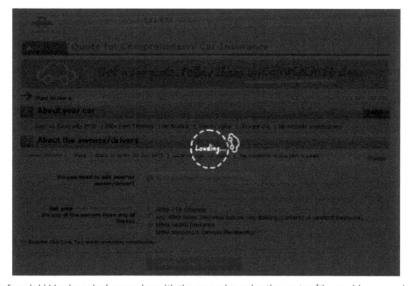

5-51. This form is hidden by a shadow overlay, with the processing animation on top (the car drives around the circle)

If you do use popups and overlays, though, make sure they're coded accessibly.

Regardless, you should always disable the primary action button for the form, so it can't be accidentally submitted twice:

5-52. There's no pushing this button twice

From Good to Great

Let's review the book so far.

You've written good questions and put them in the right order. You've structured the form into well laid out and visually pleasing screens, and are communicating clearly with the user through carefully designed messages. You're using validation to catch a number of mistakes before the form is submitted, and treating the user as an intelligent partner in their resolution.

You could stop there. After all, you've taken the basic steps to making a functional form.

But what if you wanted to create a user experience that wasn't just passable, but pleasant? Like great air conditioning, great forms disappear into the background, letting users focus on what's important.

At a minimum, to design a great form you need to:

- intelligently reduce workload
- tailor the experience.

You might be surprised to learn that both can be quite easy to do. Read on for some handy techniques.

Reduce Workload

Less work for the user means greater satisfaction.

Touch Device Smarts

Has this ever happened to you? With fat fingers and a tiny smartphone, you're trying to fill out a form. You're supposed to enter a number, but you've been given the alphabetic keyboard. You have to change the keyboard to show digits (without any mistyping).

5-53. This birthday text box accepts only digits, but an alphabetic keyboard has come up

Not a deal breaker, certainly, but a frustration nonetheless. If a numeric keyboard had come up automatically, that would make for a more seamless and less error-prone experience.

Surname

Phone Number or Email Address

Gender

Select ▼

Birthday

dd / mm / yyyy

New Password

By clicking Sign Up, you agree to our Facebook Terms and that you have read our Data Policy, including our Cookie Use. You may receive SMS Notifications from Facebook and can opt out at any time.

Sign Up

< >   Done

1	2 ABC	3 DEF
4 GHI	5 JKL	6 MNO
7 PQRS	8 TUV	9 WXYZ
+ * #	0	⌫

5-54. The birthday text box accepts only digits and shows a numeric keyboard

Simple additions to our form code can ensure that on a touch device, the right keyboard comes up for the most common field types. This not only reduces work for the user, it minimizes errors too (by limiting what can be typed). All you need to do is set the HTML input's `type` to whichever of the following options (if any) is relevant:

- `tel` (for telephone numbers)
- `email`(for email addresses)
- `url` (for web addresses)
- `cc-number` (for credit card numbers)

cc-csc (for the credit card security code)

number (for numeric inputs)

And hey presto, whenever a touch interface user enters one such type of answer field, they'll automatically get a keyboard with the right keys. Nice one!

For a full list of touch keyboard types, refer to the Baymard Institute's handy cheat sheet[5]. For more on touch, I recommend Josh Clark's excellent book *Designing for Touch*[6].

Double Entry

If you ask people what else frustrates them when filling in forms, they'll often mention having to enter their email or password not once, but twice.

Password :
Confirm password :

5-55. A not uncommon feature of sign up forms: double entry of password

This **double entry** arose in an attempt to improve the user experience, by reducing email address and password errors. The thinking was: if you ask the user to enter the information twice, and check that the two entries match, you'll pick up mistakes while the user's still there to fix them.

Unfortunately, there are lots of reasons why double entry actually makes the user experience worse:

Users will copy their entry from the first field and paste it into the second (so actually they're doing more work than a single entry, without any benefit).

If you try to prevent copy and paste by disabling it, you:

prevent the use of a password manager (thereby compromising security)

may block browser auto-fill from completing the fields (creating yet *more* work for the user).

[5.] http://baymard.com/labs/touch-keyboard-types

[6.] https://abookapart.com/products/designing-for-touch

- Having two entries that don't match doesn't tell the user which is right, so they have to enter both all over again.
- It patronizes the user, by essentially saying "you can't be trusted to enter this information correctly."

Do not ask users to enter their email address or password twice. Instead, collect this information once—like everything else on your form—and give the user a quick and simple way to reset or get a reminder. If the email address is serving as a username, or is the only way to contact the user, consider sending them an email to validate.

You can read more about double entry[7] on my blog.

[7.] http://www.formulate.com.au/blog/double-entry-form-fields

Show/hide Password

In web forms, passwords are masked as they're typed:

•••••••••

5-56. The password here is "password", but you can't tell that because it's hidden behind masking

This is to prevent the password being seen by someone nearby.

Increasingly, however, users are aware of the need to keep passwords secure from these so-called **over-the-shoulder** attacks. Also, passwords are more and more often being entered on mobile devices, which are close to the user. So the need for this protection is low, while the usability problems it causes—not being able to see what was typed—are high.

A great solution is to provide the user with the option to show their password, if they feel it's safe to do so. A simple show/hide toggle near the password field does the trick:

New password

	Show

5-57. An example of show/hide option on a password field

If you implement this feature, be sure to:

- use the words "show" and "hide" instead of (or in addition to) icons
- always start with the password hidden, which is the traditional and safer option.

For more information, see:

- "Masking passwords: help or hindrance"on SitePoint[8]
- "Why you should allow users to see their password"[9] by Josh Wayne

---

[8] https://www.sitepoint.com/masking-passwords-help-or-hindrance/
[9] https://joshwayne.com/show-password/

Pre-population

Could there be any more unnecessary workload on users than asking them to provide information they've provided before? Do whatever you can to connect up databases and services, so that **if your organization already knows something about a user, you don't end up collecting it again.**

If it provides helpful context for the user, or you want them to check it, you can present back such information in your form. This is called **pre-population**, because you're populating the fields ahead of the user.

Wherever possible, let the user update pre-populated data. When you're doing this, the pre-populated field looks like any other form field, except it has an answer in it when the screen first loads:

E-mail address:*

lucia.brown@gmail.com

Home address:*

City/Suburb/Town:*

5-58. On this form, the email address has been pre-populated

Sometimes you don't want pre-populated data to be changed via the current form. In this case, provide the pre-populated answer but remove any visual suggestion of a form field. For example, remove the border from text boxes and don't show radio buttons or check boxes:

E-mail address:*   lucia.brown@gmail.com

Home address:*

City/Suburb/Town:*

5-59. Here, the pre-populated email address cannot be changed

Defaults

A **default** is when you make a guess at what answer the user will give, and have it already provided when the form loads. Defaults are different from pre-population in an important way: they're not based on information already provided by that specific user. Instead, they're "most likely" answers.

Take the form in figure 5-60 below, for example. Three questions have default answers: "Title", "Business size" and "State and territory". The default answers will reduce workload for people who use the title "Miss" and are from small businesses in the ACT (a place in Australia). That's a good thing. But when a "Mr" with a medium sized business from NSW (a different place in Australia) comes to fill out the form, there's a high probability he'll subconsciously see those questions are already answered, and skip past them without paying any real attention. This is, in fact, what happened.

Title:	First name (required field):	Last name (required field):
Miss ▾		

Email e.g. name@domain.com (required field):	Organisation name:

Position:	Business size:
	Small (less than 20 employees) ▾

Suburb:	State or territory:	Phone:
	ACT ▾	

5-60. The owners of this form received a disproportionate number of submissions from people with the title "Miss" running small businesses in the ACT

This is very typical user behavior with forms. Remember: users are often filling out your form at the same time as cooking dinner or waiting for a bus, and they want to spend as little time and energy on it as possible. You're lucky if you have even 10% of their conscious attention.

Notice how the mistake of the "Mr" medium sized business in NSW will not be detected during validation. Maybe it won't get discovered until long after the form has been submitted, and who knows how much work that will cause—for both the user and the organization.

For this reason, **defaults are usually a bad idea**. You shouldn't even *consider* making default selections unless:

- you have data that tells you with high certainty what the answer will be, *and*
- there'll be very little impact if users don't change the answer from the default when they should.

If you do make default selections, the user *must* be able to modify them.

Tailor the Experience

Now we come to the last part of our journey from good to great: tailoring the experience to suit the user.

Perhaps you've heard people in the web world speak of "designing for delight". The idea is that you turn users into fans—fans who'll stick by your product and sing its praises—by creating delightful interactions.

I'm all for users who are fans, and for delightful interactions. But when I say "tailor the experience", I'm talking about even more basic actions. The following three actions are all aimed at avoiding more frustration for the user:

- make sure questions are relevant
- make sure the form itself is relevant and not just a waste of time
- don't let a user be kicked out of a form too soon.

Get these three things right before you worry about designing for delight.

Conditional Questions

In the tough ol' days of paper forms, we were stuck with having to include every question for every user, even if some questions only applied to some users. An example would be questions about pregnancy on a doctor's registration form, when that form is filled out by both men and women.

Sure, we could include written and graphical instructions to guide users around irrelevant questions. But these instructions are not always seen, understood or followed. And because the form has to include every question, it looks, to all users, like more work than it actually is.

One of the best features of web forms is being able to hide irrelevant questions. If users say they're male, then we never show them any of the pregnancy questions.

In this example, whether or not the pregnancy questions are shown is *conditional* on the answer to the question ascertaining sex. Thus, the pregnancy questions are **conditional questions**, and the sex question is the **trigger question**.

Here's an illustration of trigger and conditional questions in a mobile web form:

5-61. If you're taking a round or one-way trip, the form only needs to ask about two cities. This is obviously different for multi-city trips. The city questions are conditional upon the trip type trigger.

Check over your form and see if there are any questions that apply only to some users. If so, is there a *reliable* trigger question that you can use to show/hide these conditional questions? Be very careful that you get the trigger right. You don't want to lock some users out of questions that apply to them, or force irrelevant questions on some other subset of users.

Sometimes it's the answer options, not the question itself, that will be conditional. For example, car insurance quoting forms often identify the car to be insured by asking a series of questions, each of which is more narrowly focused. Later questions include answer options that are aligned with the answer to earlier trigger questions. The image below shows one such form, where Model is conditional on both Year and Make:

In what year was the car made?   2007

e.g. 2007, for a 2007 Toyota Corolla

Car make   Suzuki

Model

APV
Grand Vitara
Jimny
Liana
Swift
SX4

5-62. The "Model" question shows only those models of Suzuki that were made in 2007 for the Australian market

This is clearly much easier for the user than choosing between a giant list of every make of car that was on the market that year.

Again, you must be very careful not to make it impossible for the user to answer accurately because of the conditional setup. As I'm sure you've experienced, there's nothing quite as exasperating as wanting to give the right answer and not being able to:

Make: *

SUZUKI

Model: *

SWIFT

Year: *

-Select-

-Select-
1985

5-63. The trigger and conditional questions in this form have not been designed (or coded) correctly, preventing the user from selecting the appropriate year (2007)

Eligibility

If your form as a whole may not be applicable to some users, it's good to screen these users out via some **eligibility** questions.

In the state where I live, residents who have issues related to buying and selling can raise those issues with an organization called Consumer Affairs Victoria (CAV). However, state law prohibits CAV from investigating a complaint until the buyer and the seller have tried to resolve it themselves. These and other restrictions determine eligibility for CAV's online complaint form, and are queried up front:

General complaint

Questions   Your details   Company de

Questions

All fields are required unless marked optional.

Have you attempted to contact the trader in an attempt to solve your problem?
- ○ Yes
- ○ No

Have you lodged this complaint with the Victorian Civil and Administrative Tribunal (VCAT) or a court?
- ○ Yes
- ○ No

Are you a trader making a complaint against another trader?
- ○ Yes
- ○ No

Is your dispute regarding a private sale?
- ○ Yes
- ○ No

Have you lodged this complaint with another organisation, such as an ombudsman?
- ○ Yes
- ○ No

Next   Cancel

5-64. Eligibility questions for Consumer Affairs Victoria's online complaint form

If the user's answers indicate that the form doesn't apply to them, they are told this immediately:

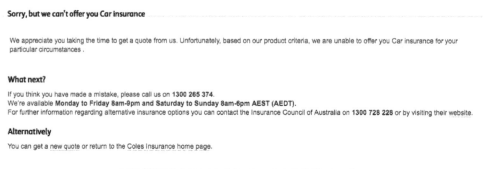

General complaint

| Questions | Your details | Company details | Problem/evidence details | Review and submit |

Questions

All fields are required unless marked optional.

Have you attempted to contact the trader in an attempt to solve your problem?

○ Yes
◉ No

ⓘ Consumer Affairs Victoria is unable to conciliate complaints until you have contacted the trader about a problem. If, after you have contacted the trader, you feel that our assistance is required, please feel free to contact us again. Alternatively, you may wish to alert Consumer Affairs Victoria to an emerging scam, by using the Dob in a Scam form.

Have you lodged this complaint with the   ○ Yes

5-65. The user is told immediately when their answer means they are ineligible

When the user is ineligible, you should also make it impossible to proceed with the form. Ideally, this is done by presenting a message upon submission of the eligibility page:

Sorry, but we can't offer you Car insurance

We appreciate you taking the time to get a quote from us. Unfortunately, based on our product criteria, we are unable to offer you Car insurance for your particular circumstances .

What next?

If you think you have made a mistake, please call us on **1300 265 374**.
We're available **Monday to Friday 8am-9pm and Saturday to Sunday 8am-6pm AEST (AEDT)**.
For further information regarding alternative insurance options you can contact the Insurance Council of Australia on **1300 728 228** or by visiting their website.

Alternatively

You can get a new quote or return to the Coles Insurance home page.

5-66. Message appearing after insurance eligibility questions

Unlike disabling the submit button, this approach ensures the user is never left unable to proceed without knowing why. And it's obviously a better approach than allowing the user to go to all the effort of filling in the form anyway, only to get rejected at the end.

If you do have eligibility questions, a good place for them is between your gateway screen and the rest of the form. Be open with users about the purpose of the step, especially if it includes questions that may otherwise seem unrelated.

Time Limits

Some forms have time limits. While these limits can be good for security and performance, they can also be extremely annoying if implemented poorly. For instance, imagine you've almost finished filling in a multi-step form, when you pause to answer a phone call. After the call is done, you look back to the screen to see a message like this:

Session Timeout

You have exceeded the inactivity limit set for the interflora.com.au site and for security reasons you have been logged out of the system. To continue with your visit please click the 'RESTART' link below. You will need to start your ordering process again as all previous information has been discarded.

Thank you for visiting the Interflora Web Site.

Your shopping session will log out automatically 15 minutes after your last page request.

Restart

5-67. Returning to a form only to see a message like this can be infuriating

Follow these four simple steps for improving user experience with time limits:

1. The time limit should be at least 20 minutes.
2. Give the user plenty of warning when the time is running low.
3. Always allow the time to be extended by *at least* the length of the original limit.
4. In multi-step forms, start counting down from when each step is loaded, not from the beginning of the form as a whole.

Here's an illustration of an ideal time limit message and process:

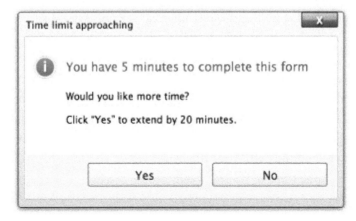

5-68. A much better approach to time limits: plenty of warning and ability to extend, all communicated in plain English

Unfortunately, most time limits fail to do some or all of these things. To make matters worse, they rarely follow the recommendations for writing good messages, using jargon like "session", "inactivity", "expire" and "reset":

5-69. This time limit has been implemented poorly. Even the buttons are in the wrong order! How many improvements could you make?

The Art and Science of Flow

Flow is about recognizing that *humans* are filling out our forms, not computers. Sequence, tone and effort all really matter to humans.

Using the analogy of a conversation to help guide our design decisions, you saw the importance of:

- devising an appropriate order—for questions and screens—by understanding the user's perspective and looking for natural groupings
- creating a suitable gateway before the form, and confirmation after the form
- keeping the user informed, through progress indicators and messages, which have the right visuals and text
- reducing workload through:
  - touch device smarts
  - avoiding double entry
  - pre-populating with information we already have
  - being wise about defaults
- tailoring the form to user needs, by:
  - using conditional and trigger questions
  - checking eligibility
  - handling time limits well.

The first section of this chapter, Order, showed just how much designing a great **flow** is both an art and a science. This message was reinforced by acknowledging the following:

- gateway pages are not always needed, nor are they always distinct from the start of the form
- progress indicators may also not be needed
- validation takes real time to design, and if done poorly can actually interrupt and confuse
- defaults and pre-population can actually *increase* errors.

Hopefully I've given enough information about each component to guide you in the right direction with your forms—with *your* target audience, in *your* context. And by now you know that user research is always there to help.

Happy designing!

Appendix A: Forms Documentation: QxQ

Even if your team is using an agile or lean approach, forms are complex yet so influential that they need some documentation. Otherwise, you'll have people asking you, a year from now, why one question isn't included and another is asked the way it is.

The most efficient and effective form documentation is a **QxQ**, which stands for "Question by Question". A QxQ records information about the questions in a form, to assist both current and future design, development and decision-making. It can be prepared as a document or a spreadsheet, whatever you find easiest.

Contents of a QxQ

The content of a QxQ can vary depending on the context of use, but I recommend the following for each question:

- the proposed question, namely:
  - label
  - question-level help
  - answer field, including
    - whether answering is required or optional
    - whether open or closed
    - if closed:
      - what type (checkboxes, radio buttons, date picker etc.)
      - the answer options, in order
      - whether the answer options are based on, or exactly match, a standard (e.g. ISO 5218: international codes for representing sex electronically, or AS4590: the Australian standard for addresses)
      - whether the user is allowed to choose more than one option
      - if there's an "other" option, whether the user needs to write in their other answer
    - if open:

- the minimum and maximum number of characters the answer must be, if any (e.g. for an email address: minimum of 3 characters, maximum of 256 characters)
- which characters need to be accepted (e.g. all alphanumeric characters plus apostrophes, dollar signs, hyphens and spaces)
- relevant HTML5 form input type e.g. `tel`, `email` or `date`
- whether question is a determinant of eligibility
- any useful notes about the proposed wording, including relevant findings from user research
- validation rules, such as allowable minimums and maximums for numbers or dates
- relationship to other questions, e.g. conditional or trigger
- to which users the question is applicable
- who will use the data from the question, and how
- any relevant history.

 Simple Forms Don't Need a QxQ

It's probably not worth doing a QxQ for very short or simple forms.

QxQs are sometimes called **question protocols**, but the term "protocol" can mean something slightly different in different domains, so I prefer QxQ.

The Investment in a QxQ Has a Great Return

It may seem like a lot of work, but you'll find the QxQ immensely valuable. It presents the content of the form separately from its code. This makes it simpler to:

- evolve the code over time (e.g. change to a different framework)
- evolve the content over time (e.g. add, remove and modify questions).

As time passes, the people working on the form will change. A QxQ expedites the handover process and retains important organizational knowledge.

As the form's designer, people will look to you for the background to the form. It's incredibly helpful to be able to point to a record, especially one which documents the rationale behind question changes.

Finally, a QxQ assists development. It prompts us to consider all of the elements of the design that the developer needs to know. By streamlining this aspect of development, we conserve resources for more difficult, form-related challenges.

9 780994 347053